7/07 OX

JUN 1 3 2002

THE DICTIONARY OF
Religion

Robert S. Ellwood, Ph.D.

Professor Emeritus, University of Southern California
General Editor

Gregory D. Alles, Ph.D.

Western Maryland College

Marilee Foglesong

Former Young Adult Coordinator, The New York Public Library

Neil Gillman, Ph.D.

Jewish Theological Seminary of America

Advisers

Franklin Watts
A Division of Scholastic Inc.
New York   Toronto   London   Auckland   Sydney
Mexico City   New Delhi   Hong Kong
Danbury, Connecticut

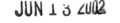

DEVELOPED, DESIGNED, AND PRODUCED BY
BOOK BUILDERS LLC

Photographs © **Aboriginal Fine Arts Gallery, NT Australia:** 13; **Archive Photos:** 10, 49; 9, 16, 50, 93, 99, 115 (Hutton Getty/Archive); 21 (Santi Visalli, Inc.); 74 (Reuters/Jayanta Shaw/Archive Photos); 108 (Reuters/Michael De Mocker/Archive Photos); **British Tourism Authority:** 34 *top*; **Robert Burch Communications:** 34 *bottom*; **China Span:** 78 (Keren Su), 113; **Concordia College, Language Villages, Moorhead, MN:** 71; **Corbis Images:** cover *top second left*, cover *top second right*, cover *top far right*, 22 *right*; **Culver Pictures:** 11, 15 *right*, 23, 28, 54, 90; courtesy of **Roshan Rivetna, ed., Fezana Journal:** 122; **Danny and Julie Han, Tenafly, NJ:** 119; **Heartsong Church, Cordova, TN:** 92; **Dr. Abdul Jandali and Ameena Jandali:** 94; **Michael Meyers:** 75; **National Museum of the American Indian, Smithsonian Institution:** 112 *left* (Fred E. Miller); **Photo Researchers:** 43 (Bill Aron); 91 (G. Aschendorf Agence Vandystadt); 57 (Mehmet Biber); 15 *left* (Donna Bise); 116 (Van Bucher); 67 (Carl Frank); 14 (David R. Frazier); 61 (Gordon Gahan); 26 (Farrel Grehan); 25, 65 (Eunice Harris); 38 (Bruce Hayes); 42 (George Holton); 55 (Alok Kavan); 8 (Susan Kuklin); 64 (Jan Lukas); 69 (Rafael Macia); 80 (George and Judy Manna); 121 (Susan McCartney); 103 (Will & Deni McIntyre); 76 (Lawrence Migdale); 97 (Joseph Nettis); 31 (Kazuyoshi Nomachi); 22 *left* (Harry Rogers); 20 (Stephen L. Saks); 95, 98 (Blair Seitz); 32 (Jean-Gérard Sidaner); 85 *left* (Paul Stepan); 117 (Tetrel); 109 (David Weintraub); **Oral Roberts Ministries:** 48; **SEF/Art Resource, NY:** cover *bottom*; **Skokomish Indian Tribe Museum, Shelton WA:** 88 (Andy Wilbur, artist); **St. John Theologian Greek Orthodox Cathedral, Tenafly, NJ:** 85 *right*; **Suri Family, Tenafly, NJ:** 101; **Malcom Varon:** cover *top far left*, 112 *right*; **Wildlife Conservation Society:** 6 (Diane Shapiro); **Jim and Mary Whitmer:** 40, 45. Cover and interior design by **Ann Antoshak** for Book Builders.

Every endeavor has been made to obtain permission to use copyrighted material. The publishers would appreciate errors or omissions being brought to their attention.

Library of Congress Cataloging-in-Publication Data

The dictionary of religion.
    p. cm. (Watts reference)
  "A Watts reference book."
  Includes bibliographical references and index.
  ISBN 0-531-11982-3
  1. Religions--Dictionaries, Juvenile. [1. Religions—Encyclopedias.] I. Series.

BL92 .D53 2001
200'.3--dc21   00-065424

Contents

Note to the Reader

This book is an invitation to explore the world of religion. Religion is the way in which people worship God, the gods, or what they feel to be the highest wisdom—whatever they see as most powerful.

Religion is one of the most important areas of human life. It influences how people organize their societies and their own lives. In studying religion, you will learn about the customs and cultures of different people in numerous regions of the United States and the world. As you gain an understanding of others, you may begin to reflect on what is important to you.

Religion is many things, from deep inner thoughts to popular celebrations like Christmas and Halloween. It is a history of great men and women who have founded religions or changed religious life. It is the story of human life lived in dramatically different ways—from those of a single family to the ways of monks and nuns.

Let this dictionary lead your exploration. Look up alphabetically what you need to research. Discover interesting details in the "Holiday" and "Life of" boxes. The index also can guide you, and other books will take you further. Always keep exploring.

How to Use This Book

The topics in the *Dictionary of Religion* are arranged in alphabetical order, from A to Z. They identify and explain a variety of subjects related to the world's religions and the practices and customs of those religions. You will find that the longest entries in the dictionary center on the religious and cultural traditions that are most common in each region of the United States, and the world. Look for these entries: Midwestern U.S., Northeastern U.S., Pacific Northwest, Southern U.S., Southwestern U.S., Australia and the Pacific Islands, Canada, East Asia, Europe, India and South Asia, the Middle East, North America, Mexico and Central America, and South America.

Scattered throughout the dictionary are lightly colored boxes with special features. "Holidays" highlight how people of different religions celebrate certain sacred or special days. "Life of" features focus on key people—some who founded a major world religion and others who have played historic roles in a particular religion. You also will find some topics that have only a title and a line that directs you to "see" another topic. These directions send you to where the topic is fully discussed.

Most topics, or entries, in the dictionary contain cross-references. These are words or phrases in SMALL CAPITAL LETTERS that point you to related subjects discussed elsewhere in the dictionary. Whenever you see a cross-reference, in either the text or at the end of an entry, you can find additional information on that topic in a separate entry. At the back of the book, the index also will help you locate topics, and the list of books and websites will further expand your search.

Note to the Educator

Although the *Dictionary of Religion* serves as a general reference for the basic terms, concepts, and main traditions of religion, it also contains special articles on the cultural nature of religion in major geographical areas of the United States and the world. While different religions or denominations with different beliefs may exist in, say, India or the southern United States, those religions may share some similar customs. Such "family resemblances" remind us that a region can have a common religious "style." For example, in the American South, the gospel music of the Baptists is very similar in style to the gospel music of the Seventh Day Adventists.

Like learning to connect with different cultures by finding some common ground (the French Bastille Day celebrations are like the American Fourth of July festivities), researching different religions can teach young people not only to appreciate and respect the differences among faiths but also identify the sometimes similar customs that can arise from geographic proximity.

We hope that this dictionary will help young readers begin to explore the role of religion in human history. We also hope that recognizing religious and cultural similarities among different groups will lead them to better appreciating their differences.

Robert S. Ellwood, *General Editor*

AFRICA (SUB-SAHARAN) 🌿

Africa south of the Sahara desert. Today most Africans—black and white—practice either CHRISTIANITY or ISLAM. Some Africans, mostly black, practice traditional African religions. These are the religions that Africans practiced before most of them converted to Islam or Christianity. Africans of Indian (South Asian) descent preserve their Hindu heritage. They generally live along the coasts of eastern and southern Africa.

Africans have adopted Christianity or Islam for many reasons. Not all of them have been religious. For example, some Africans associate CHRISTIANITY with colonialists from EUROPE and NORTH AMERICA. They sometimes say that they prefer ISLAM, in part because it is a religion native to their part of the world. Other Africans, however, have converted to one or another tradition of Christianity precisely because they see it as European or North American. For example, in the 1990s people on the Cape Verde islands, off the coast of western Africa, were converting to PROTESTANTISM. They said that they hoped doing so would make them rich like North Americans.

Today, only about 10 percent of Africans practice African traditional religions, but these religions have left their mark on Islam and Christianity in Africa. African Independent Churches are good examples. Native Africans, rather than missionaries from Europe and America, started these churches. Their teachings and styles of worship resemble traditional beliefs, art, and music.

Africans who came to the Americas as slaves brought African traditional religions with them. These religions formed the basis of religions like VOODOO in Haiti, Santeria in Cuba, and Candomble in Brazil. Immigrants brought all three of these religions to the United States.

Heroes and Saints. PROPHETS have been important religious leaders in Africa. Some prophets have started African Independent Churches. For example, a prophet named Isaiah Shembe founded the Zulu ama-Nazaretha Church in South Africa. Another named Simon Kimbangu

Masks

Africans have traditionally used masks for religious purposes. Based on long-standing stories, many Africans believe there are beings in the world, like spirits and ANCESTORS, whom we cannot see. The use of masks makes it possible to visualize those beings. Masks make the spirits present in rituals in a special way, so that people can interact with them.

Masks can take many forms. Some masks made by the Igbo of Nigeria sit on top of the head; the face of the wearer is covered with a cloth. Among the subjects portrayed in these masks is a white person—indeed a colonial ruler whom the Igbo have given a part in a ritual drama. Masks can be made out of many different materials, too. Many masks are wooden. In Benin only royalty could use bronze and ivory masks.

Today, Africans do not make masks only for religious purposes. They also make them as works of art and as souvenirs to sell to tourists.

Masks have special religious meaning in certain African traditions.

founded "The Church of Jesus Christ on Earth Through the Prophet Simon Kimbangu" in central Africa. Both of these prophets combined Christian and traditional African elements in their teachings. They both also gave special attention to healing.

Other African religious leaders practice healing, too. That is because they often believe disease has spiritual causes. According to some African traditions, people get sick because spirits have taken control of them. To others, however, disease comes from WITCHCRAFT, the power of one person to make another person sick. Some Africans believe that witches perform RITUALS to make people sick. Others say that people get sick just from being around a witch, even if the witch does not actually do anything.

Traditional leaders called diviners tell people why they are sick or suffering—for example, what witch has made them sick—and what they can do to get better. Healers use traditional medicines and techniques, including rituals, to offset witchcraft and evil spirits.

Another important class of religious figures in Africa is the ANCESTORS. Ancestors include parents, grandparents, and other relatives who have died. They also include the first beings in stories about creation. People remember the ancestors. They also pray to them and give them OFFERINGS. They expect to get good things in return. In fact, although many traditional African religions have recognized one highest God, Africans have often expected greater rewards from ancestors and other spirits. They believe that God is too far away to pay much attention to them.

Art and Music. Africans have produced much beautiful art and music. Some MISSIONARIES taught native Africans that to be good Christians, they had to give up African ways. As a result, some African Christians are reluctant to use African music in their worship. Others use both native music and dance.

African art often has religious significance. That may be true of the ancient rock paintings of the San people in South Africa. It is certainly true of many, but not all, of the masks that are made today. In addition, African artists have produced artwork that reflects Christianity and Islam. For example, Christian artists have produced paintings and sculptures based on stories from the Bible. [*See also* HINDUISM.]

AFRICAN AMERICAN RELIGIONS

The religions of people of African descent in the Americas today. African Americans practice a wide variety of religious traditions, but are mostly Protestant Christians. In the late seventeenth century, when most African Americans were enslaved, a free man, Richard Alan, founded the first independent African American church. It was called the African Methodist Episcopal Church, or A.M.E. Historically, African American churches are cultural and political centers in African American communities. The civil rights leader, the Reverend Dr. Martin Luther King, Jr. used churches all over the country to rally people together for equal rights. Not all African Americans are Christians, however. Many are Muslims. For example, Malcolm X belonged to the

Kwanzaa

An African American HOLIDAY. Kwanzaa is a seven-day celebration that starts on December 26 and ends on January 1. People exchange gifts on each of the seven days. Each day has a different African name, which stands for the seven important principles of Kwanzaa. The seven days are:

Umoja—unity
Kujichagulia—self-determination
Ujima—collective work and responsibility
Ujamaa—cooperative economics
Nia—purpose
Kuumba—creativity
Imani—faith

Each of these seven principles is important to the African American community. African Americans do not celebrate this holiday as a replacement for Christmas. Instead, they celebrate Kwanzaa to remind them of their African heritage and of their present-day lives in NORTH AMERICA.

Nation of ISLAM, an African American Muslim group. [*See also* CHRISTIANITY; PROTESTANTISM; SOUTHWESTERN UNITED STATES.]

African Americans share their heritage.

AFTERLIFE ⚜ The continuation of life after death. Each culture and religion has teachings about what happens after a person dies. Followers of ISLAM and CHRISTIANITY believe that after death, a person will face judgment by God for their deeds. HINDUISM and BUDDHISM emphasize REINCARNATION. The greatest souls, however, will be absorbed into the Supreme reality, *Brahman Nirvana*. Many cultures make special preparations for the afterlife. For example, ancient Egyptians made mummies to preserve a person's body. Some NATIVE AMERICAN groups buried their dead facing the western setting sun. Modern FUNERALS show the same care and respect for those setting out on a journey into the afterlife.

AGNOSTICISM ❧ *See* ATHEISM.

ALLAH ❧ *See* ISLAM.

ALTAR ❧ A table or raised platform used during religious services. SACRIFICES are offered to God from the altar. In some religions, however, no altars are used. Other religions use altars with RELIGIOUS ART, such as the beautifully carved altars to Zeus or the elaborate altars of HINDUISM. Altars can be built in private homes or public places. They can be fixed in place or movable. Some altars are designed to hold a RELIC. [*See also* TEMPLE; WORSHIP.]

AMISH ❧ A Protestant group living mostly in farm communities in Pennsylvania and in the midwest United States. They are very at-

The Amish believe in leading simple lives.

tached to their traditional way of life, and they try to keep apart from other communities and practices. For example, many use horse-drawn buggies instead of automobiles, and hooks-and-eyes instead of zippers. Some refuse to vote. In their devotion to peaceful and gentle ways, they often refuse military service. To preserve their special religious beliefs, they refuse to send their children to public schools after the eighth grade. The United States Supreme Court has upheld this right. [*See also* PROTESTANTISM.]

ANALECTS OF CONFUCIUS ❧ A collection of sayings gathered by the first followers of Confucius, the great Chinese philosopher. Confucius, who lived about 550–480 B.C.E, did not put his principles into writing. But the Analects are believed to be best source of information on his life and teachings. The *Analects* have had enormous influence on China all through history. One of the main teachings of Confucius reported in the Analects is a deep respect for parents, whether or not they are still living. [*See also* CONFUCIANISM; PHILOSOPHY.]

ANCESTORS ❧ Persons from whom one is descended, like a grandparent or great-grandparent. Many people, including Africans, Asians, Native Americans, and the native people of Australia, believe that the SPIRITS of their ancestors help them in everyday life. These people practice ancestor WORSHIP to honor the spirits of their ancestors. Ancestor worship may include special PRAYER, celebration, storytelling, FUNERALS, visiting cemetaries and SACRIFICE. For example, the Chinese New Year is a special time for ancestor worship. The Chinese set off loud firecrackers and offer red dates, winter melon, peanut candy, and other sweets to the spirits of their ancestors. [*See also* AUSTRALIA AND THE PACIFIC ISLANDS; CONFUCIANISM; NATIVE AMERICAN RELIGIONS.]

ANGEL ✧ A spiritual messenger or servant of God. Angels are important in Western religions such as JUDAISM, CHRISTIANITY, and ISLAM. Sometimes angels are grouped into ranks. The three most familiar ranks are called seraphim, cherubim, and archangels. Each rank of angel performs a special task. Angels may also be objects of devotion, but not of worhsip. That means people pray to certain angles for special reasons. For many people, angels represent a warm, guiding, and protecting presence.

ANGLICANISM ✧ The DOCTRINE and religious practices of the Church of England and other churches that follow its practices, such as the Episcopal Church. The Church of England officially separated from the authority of the POPE in 1534. The practices and beliefs of Anglicanism share some features of ROMAN CATHOLICISM and PROTESTANTISM. Women are allowed to serve as priests and bishops. Anglicanism is known for stately and colorful worship and for tolerance of a variety of beliefs and styles of service.

ANIMALS ✧ *See* BIRDS; CATS; SNAKE.

ANIMISM ✧ The belief that everything has a SOUL or SPIRIT living in it. In animism, even trees, MOUNTAINS, rivers, the SUN, the MOON, and so on, are thought to have a soul or spirit living in them. Animism helps explain why people in some religions pray to the things of NATURE. Animism also used to be a way of explaining how religion

Angel shown on a stained-glass window

began. [*See also* DEMONS; DRUIDS; FOLK RELIGION; NATIVE AMERICAN RELIGIONS; NATURE; STAR; TIBET.]

APOCALYPSE ✳ *See* END OF THE WORLD.

APOSTLES ✳ The 12 DISCIPLES, or close followers, of JESUS CHRIST. The BIBLE tells that they were sent by Jesus to preach and to heal the sick in his name. Their missions brought many people to CHRISTIANITY. They have great authority in Christian churches because they actually saw and lived with Jesus. According to tradition, some apostles went to distant lands. St. Thomas is said to have gone to India. St. Peter went to Rome and was, in the view of Roman Catholics, the first POPE. Letters of

Jesus taught humility by washing his disciples' feet.

the apostles, called *epistles*, are found in the NEW TESTAMENT. St. Paul is often called an apostle, but he was not among the 12 close followers of Jesus. [*See also* DISCIPLES; NEW TESTAMENT.]

ART, RELIGIOUS ✳ Any artwork that has religious meaning. Religious art may be paintings, sculpture, architecture, stained glass, or poetry. Religious art may tell the stories of a religion, as do the IMAGES showing the life of JESUS CHRIST. Art may also be an object of worship. For example, Buddhists pray to the statue of Buddha. Some religions, such as ISLAM, have strict rules about art. They do not want their members to worship a sacred statue instead of God. In these cases, they may decorate religious buildings with geometric painting or abstract SYMBOLS.

ASTRONOMY ✳ *See* SCIENCE.

ATHEISM ✳ The belief that there is no God. There have been atheists in all cultures. People are atheists for different reasons. For example, they do not believe a good God could have made a world with as much evil in it as this one. Or they believe that science can give all the answers about life, and that people can live a good life without God. Many atheists are humanists. Humanists stress the good of people, rather than having faith in God. Agnosticism is the view of someone who neither believes nor disbelieves in God. Agnostics usually say that there is no way to decide if there is a God.

AUSTRALIA AND THE PACIFIC ISLANDS ✤

The Pacific Ocean is dotted with groups of islands such as Hawaii, Melanesia, and Polynesia. At the south of this vast region are the islands of New Zealand. To the far southwest is the continent of Australia.

Today the major religion of this region is CHRISTIANITY because Christian missionaries worked very hard in this part of the world. The first missionaries came from EUROPE in the 1700s. Soon, however, people from the islands themselves became missionaries and spread Christianity to other islands. About one-third of the people practice ROMAN CATHOLICISM. The rest practice some form of PROTESTANTISM.

Before Europeans came, the native peoples, or peoples already living in the region, had their own religions. These religions have not disappeared. In some places they are still strong, as in the less settled parts of Australia. In other places some beliefs of local religions became part of Christian practice.

Styles of Worship. Native religions in Australia and the Pacific Islands used many different RITUALS. Some people in the Pacific Islands SACRIFICED pigs or other animals to

Initiations of Young Men

Many religions mark the time when people become adults with rituals. Examples include the BAR AND BAT MITZVAH in JUDAISM, CONFIRMATION in ROMAN CATHOLICISM, BAPTISM in some forms of PROTESTANTISM, and the Quinceañera in MEXICO AND CENTRAL AMERICA.

In Australia and the Pacific Islands the initiation of young men has been especially important. That is because through initiation the young men became members of secret societies. These societies had their own special knowledge and rituals. The rituals had to be performed just right if the world was going to continue to do well.

During the initiation boys sometimes had to go off and live apart from the rest of the group. During this time they learned the secret knowledge of the group. Initiations often required changes to the body, too. One of the most common was CIRCUMCISION. In some places initiation was thought of as dying to childhood and being reborn to manhood.

their ANCESTORS to make their crops grow. In Australia, native people use rituals to keep the world working. Their rituals re-create the Dreaming, or mythical time of creation. However, native Australians do not use PRAYER.

Death and Funerals. Native religions in Australia and the Pacific Islands have well-developed initiations for young men. They also have complex death rituals. In some places initiations and funeral rituals go together.

Native funeral rituals often dealt with death very differently from what is common in North America. For example, one group of people in Borneo put the corpse on display for as long as six years. In many places it was common to gather the bones of the dead and wash them. In Polynesia people celebrated the funerals of dead people of high status by holding elaborate feasts and sometimes mutilating themselves.

Ethics. In parts of Australia and the Pacific Islands, traditional customs were important. People had to

The dilly bag is a popular kind of Aborigine art.

be very careful of how they treated other people and things. For example, some men had to avoid their mothers-in-law. Common people had to keep their distance from a king. Some people were supposed to avoid certain foods. Things and people that a person had to avoid were called *tapu*. This has given us the English word TABOO.

Art. Australia and the Pacific Islands have produced a great amount of religious art. One good example is the giant stone sculptures on Easter Island. Some of them are 40 feet (12 meters) tall.

But some very beautiful religious art from this region is fragile and does not last very long at all. Some examples are masks, paintings on bark, and carved canoes.

AUTHORITY, RELIGIOUS

People who decide the beliefs and practices for the followers of a particular religious tradition. This authority can be in written rules or books, such as the SCRIPTURES. Or individuals with special training, such as RABBIS or PRIESTS, or people who have a special connection to a god, such as PROPHETS, GURUS, or SHAMANS may hold religious authority. Disagreements over types of religious authority can sometimes lead religious traditions to split into DENOMINATIONS. [*See also* BIBLE; DOCTRINE; LAW, RELIGIOUS; PREACHER.]

B

BAHA'I ❧ A religion that arose in the mid-nineteenth century C.E. in Iran. It was founded by Baha u'llah (1817–1892). The main teaching of Baha'i is that God sent a series of great PROPHETS, including Jesus and Muhammad. The latest prophet is Baha u'llah. His central message is that God and the world are one. Baha'i has spread around the world. [*See also* CHRISTIANITY; ISLAM.]

Baha'i temple near Chicago, Illinois

BAPTISM ❧ One of the RITUALS of CHRISTIANITY. It is the ceremony by which a person accepts Christ and joins the church. The ritual of baptism is not the same in every denomination, but it usually involves water. This is a SYMBOL that he or she has been cleansed from sin. In some DENOMINATIONS, the ritual of baptism is performed on newborn babies. In others, only adults are baptized.

BAPTISTS ❧ Members of the Baptist Church. They follow the beliefs of PROTESTANTISM but hold special beliefs about BAPTISM. Only those members who are old enough to decide for themselves if they accept Christ are baptized. The RITUAL involves immersing the believer completely under water. Baptists are a major group in the SOUTHERN UNITED STATES. In general, Baptist services center around SERMON, PRAYER, and HYMN singing.

Celebrating Baptism by immersion in water

BAR/BAT MITZVAH ❧ The name given to Jewish children when they take on the adult responsibility of keeping the commandments. Bar Mitzvah means son of the commandment and Bat Mitzvah means daughter of the commandment. At young adulthood—12 for girls, 13 for boys—Jewish children become responsible for performing Jewish RITUALS commanded by the TORAH and TALMUD. Usually a Bar or Bat Mitzvah celebrates this RITE OF PASSAGE by reading from the TORAH in the SYNAGOGUE, by saying special prayers, and sometimes also by having a party, also called a Bar/Bat Mitzvah, with family and friends. [*See also* JUDAISM.]

BHAGAVAD GITA ❧ The "Song of the Lord," a long poem in the Sanskrit language, and the most important writing in HINDUISM. It consists of a talk between KRISHNA, who is a god in human form, and a warrior, Arjuna. The *Bhagavad Gita* is mostly about war and duty, but it also reports Krishna's declaration that he is the highest of the gods. [*See also* SCRIPTURES.]

BIBLE ❧ In JUDAISM and CHRISTIANITY, the book of sacred SCRIPTURES. The Jewish Bible, or Hebrew scriptures, contains the story of God's CREATION of the world and the early history of the Israelites. This part of the Bible centers on the call of Abraham, the Israelites' exodus out of Egypt, and the giving of the TEN

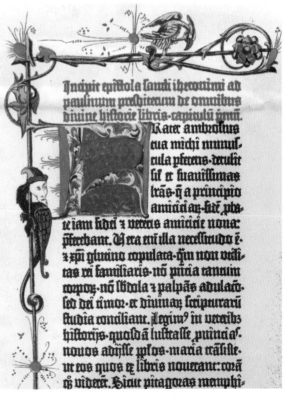

Johann Gutenburg printed this Latin Bible in the 1450s.

COMMANDMENTS to Moses on Mt. Sinai. Jews call this part of the Bible the TORAH. Later parts of the Bible give more history, poetry (the psalms), and the teachings of the prophets. Christians call this part of the Bible the Old Testament. Christians add a second part, called the NEW TESTAMENT. It tells of the life of Jesus and the early Christian church.

BIRDS ✤ A feathered animal associated with GODS, SPIRITS, and heavenly messengers throughout history. The bird has religious meaning for many cultures. For example, the ancient Egyptian sun GODS, Re and Horus, are pictured as hawks. The ancient Greeks believed that the owl was the favorite bird of their goddess of wisdom, Athena. Greek armies took an owl to war with them. People have also seen birds as messengers from heaven. In the BIBLE, a dove brought proof back to Noah that the flood was over. [*See also* CIVILIZATIONS, ANCIENT.]

BLESSINGS ✤ The act of calling on God or a spiritual being to give protection or help. Priests and ministers often give a blessing to people or things. For example, a priest might offer blessings for the sick or the poor. Certain blessings occur at fixed times of the year such as on feast-days or holidays. The word *blessing* also refers to a gift from God. Thus, one might say that good health is a blessing from God.

BUDDHISM ✤ A religion that began in Asia about 560 B.C.E. The founder of Buddhism was called the Buddha, which means an awakened or enlightened being. Thus, the Buddha has waken up and realized what life and the universe were about, why people suffer, and how people can stop suffering. People suffer, the Buddha

A golden Buddha in the country of Bhutan, north of India

said, because they want things and cling to them. But things can never satisfy people's deepest needs.

Teachings. The Buddha teaches that not seeing things as they really are will lead to suffering. The Buddha teaches people how to *wake up* through MEDITATION.

Practices. Because it is a religion some 2,500 years old, Buddhism is practiced in many ways in keeping with different traditions. Still, its various practices teach one benefit: learning how to know who we really are.

The school called Theravada, or the way of the elders, found in South Asia, teaches basic meditation methods and how to make good KARMA. It is led by MONKS who follow the Buddha's path full time. Mahayana Buddhism is found in such countries as China, Korea, Japan, and Vietnam. It teaches that people are already enlightened beings, but do not realize it.

Zen Buddhism teaches a certain form of quiet meditation in which the realization can be awakened. Nichiren Buddhism has people find harmony with the enlightened vibrations of the universe by chanting. Pure Land Buddhism teaches people to realize their *Buddha-nature* by faith. Vajravana Buddhism, found in Tibet and Mongolia, uses complex RITUALS and meditation to bring out people's true nature. [*See also* INDIA AND SOUTH ASIA.]

The Life of Buddha (560–480 B.C.E.)

It is said that the Buddha, Siddhartha Guatama, lived in ancient India. His father was a king who kept from him all sight of suffering, poverty, and DEATH. But when Siddhartha was a young man, he saw four things that were new to him: an aged man, a dying man, a corpse, and a wandering holy man. He then knew that he must live only to learn the reason for such suffering. He left his royal surroundings and set out on a great quest.

Six years later, realizing the time had come for his ultimate breakthrough, he sat under an old tree and sank into deeper and deeper MEDITATION. Finally he understood the cause of suffering as well as the release from suffering, and found for himself full and perfect joy and peace: enlightenment. For the remaining 40 years of his life, accompanied by DISCIPLES, who later became the Buddhist order of MONKS, he traveled through India teaching this DOCTRINE.

CALVINISM ✺ A type of Protestant theology taught by John Calvin (1509–1564). Calvin emphasized that human beings cannot earn their own SALVATION. Thus, Calvinists believe in predestination. This means that some people have already been chosen by God to be saved after they die. Calvinists believe that only God's grace, or mercy, allows a person to enter heaven. The BIBLE is central to Calvinist faith and worship. The English Puritans, including the Pilgrims who came to Massachusetts in 1620, were Calvinists. Today such DENOMINATIONS as the Presbyterians, the Reformed Churches, and the United Church of Christ have a Calvinist heritage.

CANADA ✺ Canada is located north of the United States. It stretches all the way to the Arctic region. Until 1763 the French ruled much of Canada. Today, French Canadians mostly live in Quebec and the Maritime Provinces along Canada's Atlantic Coast. They are very proud of their language and culture. They mostly practice ROMAN CATHOLICISM.

In 1763 the British took Canada from the French. Canada did not become independent until 1867, but it did not fight a war in order to gain independence. As a result, the Church of England has been stronger in Canada than in the United States. It is not, however, the largest PROTESTANT group. That is the United Church of Canada. METHODISTS, CONGREGATIONALISTS, and some PRESBYTERIANS joined together to form the United Church in 1925.

Canadians take pride in being multicultural. People do not give up their old cultures to become Canadian. Instead, Canada is a patchwork of different cultures.

Some small Christian communities, like the Mennonites and the Hutterites, settled on the Great Plains in western Canada. Jews live in Canada, too. In recent years people have been bringing religions to Canada from Asia and the MIDDLE EAST, such as HINDUISM, BUDDHISM, and ISLAM. Canada is also home to many groups of native people, whom Canadians call "First Nations." They include people as diverse as the Northwest Coast Indians, the Iroquois, and the Eskimo or Inuit.

Styles of Worship. Almost half of all Canadians are Roman Catholic, and almost half of them live in French-speaking Quebec. Catholic CHURCHES celebrate Mass every day.

Among most Canadian Protestant groups, revivalism has had much less impact than it did among Protestants in the United States. As a result, there is less emphasis on an energetic, emotional worship in Canada than in the United States.

Native peoples have their own ceremonies. In a ceremony known as the potlatch, wealthy Indians on the Northwest Coast used to give others a great number of gifts and/or destroy their personal property in order to improve their standing in society. Around the Great Lakes the Iroquois traditionally give thanks to the spirits of nature at midwinter ceremonies.

Ethics. Canadians tend to take a liberal attitude toward ethics. They believe that in matters of ethics, people have a right to hold their own private opinions.

Eskimo Religion

Eskimos live in the Arctic regions of America, EUROPE, and Asia. Eskimos in Canada call themselves "Inuit," which means "the people." Today most Eskimos are Christians.

Eskimos traditionally lived by hunting animals. They have hunted land animals, sea animals, and birds. Eskimos thought of animals as related to human beings. Because they had to kill animals in order to live, they had to remain on good terms with their animal relatives. They did this by means of RITUALS. For example, the Eskimo of eastern Canada would treat a bear that they had killed as an honored guest in their settlement. The Inuit of Alaska would mourn for five days for a whale that they had killed— the same length of time that they mourned for a person who had died.

Eskimos also believed that the animals were owned by supernatural beings, especially Moon, a man, and Sedna, a woman who lived at the bottom of the ocean. If Moon or Sedna got upset, religious leaders called SHAMANS could travel to the supernatural world and try to make things better.

Nevertheless, when Canadians think about ethical questions, they often think in terms of groups. Roman Catholicism and Anglicanism stress the importance of community. The United Church of Canada stresses the need to work for social justice. Sometimes the Canadian government has treated them badly. For example, from 1876 to 1951, it was against Canadian law for people to perform native ceremonies such as the potlatch. Today the government recognizes that First Nations have a right to practice their religions.

Heroes and Saints. In 1658 François Xavier de Laval (1623–1708) became the first bishop of New France. Laval organized the Roman Catholic Church in what later became Canada. He founded a school that eventually took his name, Laval University. He commissioned artists to make some of the earlist Canadian artwork for churches.

The interior of Notre Dame, in Montreal, Canada

French Canadian Religious Culture

Many French Canadians live in the province of Quebec. They are called Quebecois. Others, called Acadians, live especially in New Brunswick.

French Canadians are strongly Roman Catholic, and their religious culture goes back to the 1600s. French Canadians tell many folk stories. Some of them are about what happens to people who do not go to confession or observe religious holidays. *Loup-garou*, or werewolves, attack such people.

French Canadian holidays have special traditions. On the Epiphany, January 6, French Canadians traditionally made a cake with a bean in it. Whoever found the bean was treated as king or queen by the rest of the family for the entire day.

Today two religious holidays are French Canadian national holidays. National Acadian Day is celebrated on August 15, the day that celebrates the Assumption of Mary, Jesus' mother, into heaven. The national holiday in Quebec is June 24, the day of St. John the Baptist. Quebecois celebrate this day with parades of floats and marching bands, traditional food, bonfires, and fireworks.

CATHEDRAL ⚜ A CHURCH that

holds the official throne of a bishop. A bishop is a person who manages or governs the churches within a particular region. Not all religions have bishops. ROMAN CATHOLICISM, ANGLICANISM, EASTERN ORTHODOXY, and some types of PROTESTANTISM have bishops, and therefore may have cathedrals. Many cathedrals are large, magnificent buildings, although a small church can also be a cathedral. A cathedral offers religious services and maintains a CONGREGATION just as any other church would. [*See also* CHURCH.]

CATHOLICISM, ROMAN ⚜

The largest branch of CHRISTIANITY. It is called Roman because its highest leader, the POPE, is located in Rome. Roman Catholic DOCTRINE is based on the Bible and Christian tradition as interpreted by Church Councils and the Pope. Catholics believe that their earthly actions can influence life after death. That is, God's mercy and FREE WILL work together toward SALVATION. Followers of Roman Catholicism recognize seven SACRAMENTS. They celebrate their beliefs in a service called a Mass. Roman Catholic worship is colorful and varied, but centers on the Eucharist. The Eucharist is the blessing of bread and wine at the celebration of Mass, as Jesus did at the Last Supper. The Catholic tradition

Basilica of the National Shrine of the Immaculate Conception, Washington, D.C.

also includes devotion to the saints, and especially to Mary, the mother of Jesus. Some of its followers live dedicated lives as MONKS AND NUNS. Today, about one-sixth of the world's population is Roman Catholic.

CATS ⚜ An animal that has played

an important role in human history and religion. The ancient Egyptians domesticated, or tamed, the cat about 4,000 years ago. Since then, the cat has become a religious SYMBOL for many cultures. The ancient Egyptians greatly honored the cat, seeing it as a symbol and companion of Bast, their GODDESS of pleasure. Some people believe that cats have supernatural powers, both good and bad. For example, in China some people associate the cat with long life, but they also believe that dead cats turn into demons. Japanese believe that it is bad luck to kill a cat. Europeans in the late Middle Ages,

Some cultures believed black cats were evil.

on the other hand, associated the cat with WITCHCRAFT and thus the DEVIL, especially a black cat.

CELIBACY ✤ The condition of not having sexual relations for religious reasons. Certain religions require some of their leaders to be celibate. For example, PRIESTS, MONKS AND NUNS, and bishops of ROMAN CATHOLICISM practice celibacy. Certain other religious people of EASTERN ORTHODOXY, BUDDHISM, and HINDUISM are also celibate. The followers of these religions feel that celibacy is a more pure way to live.

CHANTS ✤ A form of WORSHIP in which worshippers sing prayers or passages from religious books. Chants can have simple or complex music. They might be used to teach religious beliefs, as part of a RITUAL, or as a type of meditation. Certain religions have developed special chants. Two of these are the two-toned chants of Tibetan Buddhist monks, and the complicated Gregorian chants of ROMAN CATHOLICISM.

CHILDBIRTH ✤ The birth of a child is an occasion of joy, but health concerns may make it a dangerous time for both mother and child. Most religious traditions call for RITUALS of PRAYER, celebration, and PURIFICATION.

CHOIR ✤ An organized group of singers that usually performs in church services. There are many kinds of choirs. Some sing in unison without separate parts for high or low

A girls' choir

voices. Others sing multipart music. Some choirs sing a particular kind of music, such as gospel or CHANT. Still others are made up of certain types of singers, such as a men's choir or a boys' choir. A choir may take part in the church LITURGY or religious service. It may also perform religious music outside of a church.

CHRISTIANITY ✴ The religion founded by Jesus Christ. Christians believe in MONOTHEISM, that there is only one God. Christians also believe that God sent his son, Jesus Christ, for the REDEMPTION and SALVATION of humanity. Christ means MESSIAH in Greek, and Christians take their name from this title of Jesus.

History. Jesus lived and died about 2,000 years ago in the MIDDLE EAST. He preached religious renewal, performed MIRACLES, and was executed by the Romans. Christians believe that after his execution, Jesus rose from the dead. Christians call this the *Resurrection*. Jesus' first followers were Jews who spread his message around the Mediterranean world, although most of their converts were non-Jews. Within 1,000 years, most of Europe and parts of Asia and Africa were Christian.

Through their history, Christian groups who disagreed over major issues split into different DENOMINATIONS. For example, disagreements led to the split in the eleventh century between ROMAN CATHOLICISM and EASTERN ORTHODOXY. In the sixteenth century, Christians who disagreed with the authority of the POPE split off into different branches of PROTESTANTISM. Today there are many different types of Christianity all over the world. There are also NEW RELIGIOUS MOVEMENTS that combine belief in Jesus with non-Christian ideas and practices.

Practices and Beliefs. Christians believe they will achieve SALVATION through FAITH in Jesus. Some Christians show their faith by

Jesus, the founder of Christianity, preaches to his followers.

The Life of Jesus
(4 B.C.E–30 C.E.)

Jesus lived almost 2,000 years ago in Palestine, on the eastern shore of the Mediterranean Sea. Most of what people know about Jesus comes from the NEW TESTAMENT. It says that Jesus was the son of God and that his mother was a virgin named Mary.

At the age of 30 he began preaching among the Jews. Christians believe that he performed miracles, such as walking on water and raising a man from the dead. According to the New Testament, mistrustful Jews encouraged the Romans, who were in charge of Palestine, to execute Jesus by nailing him to a CROSS, known as *crucifixion*. Christians believe Jesus rose from the dead after three days and then went to HEAVEN, to God the Father. Because his followers believed he was the MESSIAH, they called him Christ, which means Messiah in Greek. Jesus' message of love and renewal spread after his death, becoming the seeds of the Christian religion.

participating in RITUALS. These include the SACRAMENTS of BAPTISM and the Eucharist, or sharing bread and wine. Others show their faith by regular attendance in CHURCH where they learn about Jesus' message. Some Christians think it is enough to follow Jesus' teachings and lead good lives. Although Christians believe there is only one God, they also believe in the TRINITY, that one God has three persons: the Father, the Son (Jesus), and the Holy Spirit.

Most Christians meet in a CHURCH on Sunday and celebrate the Eucharist. Many Christians call Sunday the Lord's day. They pray, hear readings from the BIBLE, and sometimes the church leader preaches a SERMON. Denominations have different types of leaders, such as PRIESTS, ministers, PREACHERS, bishops, or pastors.

Two important Christian FESTIVALS are Christmas, celebrating Jesus' birth, and Easter, celebrating his death and resurrection. Most Christians believe that Jesus will return at the END OF THE WORLD to take those Christians who have been saved to be with God in HEAVEN. They believe people without faith in Jesus will not be saved. Today there are almost 2 billion Christians, making Christianity one of the largest religions. [*See also* ANGLICANISM; APOSTLES; CALVINISM; CATHOLICISM, ROMAN; CHRISTIAN SCIENCE; INCARNATION; NEW RELIGIOUS MOVEMENTS; ORTHODOXY, EASTERN; PROTESTANTISM; VATICAN COUNCILS; VIRGIN BIRTH.]

CHRISTIAN SCIENCE ✄ A DENOMINATION of CHRISTIANITY founded by Mary Baker Eddy in 1879. Eddy wrote a book called *Science and Health with Key to the Scriptures* (1875). It affirms that God or Spirit alone are true reality and are perfect, with no pain or evil. Healing by changing one's perception to recognize this reality demonstrates its truth and thus is very important. So Christian Scientists use spiritual means, instead of medicine, to heal illnesses. Christian Scientists are often scorned for their rejection of medical treatment. However, in general, followers use doctors for dental work, eyeglasses, and childbirth. Christian Scientists create and maintain Reading Rooms as a means of popularizing their beliefs. Their publication, *The Christian Science Monitor*, is one of the most highly respected American newspapers.

The Christian Science Center in Boston, Massachusetts

CHURCH ✄ The building in which Christians WORSHIP. Many churches house an ALTAR on which to place OFFERINGS, and a CROSS as a SYMBOL of the death of Jesus. Churches are usually places where people can see Christian art and symbols. The word *church* can also refer to a group of worshipers. [*See also* SYNAGOGUE; TEMPLE.]

CIRCUMCISION ✄ The practice of cutting away the male foreskin. This practice usually occurs at birth or seven or eight days after birth. It may also be performed on an adult who joins a religion for which it is required. Circumcision is a religious requirement for followers of JUDAISM and ISLAM. Among Jews and Muslims, circumcision is usually a time for a celebration of the boy's entry into the religious tradition.

CITY, HOLY ✄ A city that is sacred to a religious group. A holy city may be the location of a special

building, such as the sacred Kaaba in MECCA, holy city of ISLAM. A city might be holy because of things that happened there in the past. For example, Bethlehem is holy because it is the place where Jesus was born. Jerusalem is a holy city for followers of JUDAISM, CHRISTIANITY, and ISLAM. Religious people often make PILGRIMAGES, or religious journeys, to holy cities.

CIVILIZATIONS, ANGIENT

The first civilizations arose more than 5,000 years ago in the MIDDLE EAST. About 3500 B.C.E. the Sumerian civilization emerged in southern Mesopotamia—the land between the Tigris and Euphrates rivers—today southern Iraq. About 3000 B.C.E. the Egyptian civilization emerged along the banks of the Nile. The first civilization in India had appeared by 2500 B.C.E., and in China in the second millennium (2000–1001) B.C.E. Later, in the first millennium (1–1000) B.C.E. two very important ancient civilizations arose in southern Europe—Greece and Rome.

America had ancient civilizations, too. During the first millennium (1–1000) B.C.E., the Mayan civilization flourished where southern Mexico and Guatemala are today. In the 1400s C.E. the Aztecs lived in the area of Mexico City. During the same period the Incas ruled much of the Andean region of South America.

Religion was very important to ancient civilizations. Each civilization had TEMPLES. Some scholars claim that cities first grew up around temples or ceremonial centers.

At the temples, people worshiped the God or GODS of their cities. The Sumerians and Egyptians believed that their gods lived in the temples. They gave them things to eat and drink every day. The Greeks believed that the gods visited them at special times called FESTIVALS. The Aztecs sacrificed human beings at the Great Temple in the center of their city, Tenochtitlán. They thought that these sacrifices helped give the energy of life to the gods and to the forces of nature around them.

Religion often played an important role in the governments of ancient civilizations. The Egyptians believed that their king—called Pharaoh—was a god on earth. The Romans deified their emperors—

Horus, an ancient Egyptian god, symbolized by an owl

made them into gods—after they died. Roman citizens pledged allegiance to the state by making offerings to the emperor. The Zhou emperors of China claimed to have overthrown the earlier emperors by the "Mandate of Heaven," or on the authority of God.

Except for the religions of China and India, the religions of the ancient civilizations have disappeared. In 391 C.E. the Roman emperor Theodosius outlawed all religions except CHRISTIANITY. Nevertheless, the last of the pagan temples, the temple of Isis at Philae in Egypt, did not actually shut down until about 150 years later. In the 600s C.E., most people in Egypt and Mesopotamia converted to ISLAM. When the Spaniards came to the Americas after Columbus, they converted the people to Christianity.

CLOTHING ✳ Certain clothes may have special religious meaning. All members of some traditional religious groups, like Amish Christians and Orthodox Jews, wear dress that sets them apart. For example, Amish wear "plain" clothes, with broadbrim hats for men and bonnets for women. Orthodox Jewish men may wear a skullcap and sometimes a black suit with a long black coat. In addition, persons with particular religious roles, like PRIESTS, MONKS, and NUNS, may wear special clothing. Thus, other members of the religious group know who these people are. Christian priests often wear a hard round collar. Monks and nuns are often known by long white or dark robes. Special robes or other garments may also be worn by the clergy and the CHOIR during services. These vestments add to the beauty of the service, and remind both participants and the congregation that a special activity is going on.

CLOWNS, RITUAL ✳ People who act or do tricks as part of a religious ceremony. They usually dress in unusual costumes, and often wear make up. In Bali, clowns act in rituals that purify the people and their village. Pueblo Native Americans, too, have ritural clowns, who enter a ceremony in the footsteps of the priests and humorously mimic their actions. Ritual clowns perform not for entertainment, but to contact the spiritual world. During these rituals, it is believed the spirits come down to give the people adivce and help. [See also HUMOR; NATIVE AMERICAN RELIGIONS; SOUTHWESTERN UNITED STATES.]

CONFIRMATION ✳ A religious ceremony in some Christian traditions. The ceremony confirms their belief in the religion. Often, babies who have received BAPTISM will be confirmed as young adults. Confirmation also makes young people full members of the CHURCH. In some

Christian traditions, members go through confirmation, baptism, and another ceremony called first Holy Communion all at one time. Usually a priest or bishop performs the ceremony. It involves the laying on of hands and sometimes anointing the forehead with special holy oils.

CONFUCIANISM

An approach to life based on the ideas of K'ung Fu Tzu, known in the West as Confucius. Confucius lived in ancient China (551–479 B.C.E.). His ideas have had a great impact on how the Chinese thought and lived. Today, his ideas still affect Chinese people wherever they live. Confucianism has also influenced other East Asian peoples, especially those of Japan, Korea, and Vietnam.

Confucius did not found a religion. He was interested in how people should live in this world. He wanted to help create a society where people would live together in harmony. Over time TEMPLES dedicated to Confucius were built. Some people believed he was a god. But others, especially traditional Chinese scholars, disagreed. They argued that Confucius was a sage, or a person with great wisdom.

Teachings. Confucianism teaches the importance of certain virtues, or good qualities. For example, people should be truthful and kind. In particular, they should not do things to other people that they would not like done to themselves. This last quality was called "benevolence" or "humane-ness" by Confucius.

Confucianism also teaches the importance of *li*, or proper conduct. *Li* concerns how people should act in different situations in life. For example, Confucius said people should always be respectful to those who are older than they are. Children, especially, should respect their parents.

ANCESTORS are seen as older members of a family. They, too, should be respected. So offerings of incense are made to them before a

Confucius taught people how to live.

The Life of Confucius (551–479 B.C.E.)

Confucius lived about 2,500 years ago in China. He was the founder of a system of thought named after him—CONFUCIAN-ISM. Confucius was born at a time of great disorder in China called "the Warring States Period." Different rulers were struggling for power and people were suffering.

Little is known about Confucius' early life. Stories tell us that, as a man, he tried to find work as an adviser to different rulers. He wanted to help them make good decisions to create a peaceful society. His basic teaching was that people should love one another and that rulers should be just.

His ideas about how we should live attracted many DISCIPLES to him. They believed that what Confucius said was important and they believed that his teaching could put an end to the suffering of the Warring States Period. After his death they collected his sayings in a book called the *ANALECTS OF CONFUCIUS.*

Little did he know that his ideas would guide the lives of so many millions of people.

family shrine in the home. In this way the family ancestors are helped. It is hoped that in return the ancestors will help the members of the family. People should also respect their ruler. But the ruler has a duty to be a good example for his or her subjects.

What helps people develop these good qualities? How do people learn to act properly in the world? Confucianism answers, "education." Learning helps people become better human beings. It is the way to develop moral wisdom and honesty. Confucius believed learning from the past is especially helpful. He thought that about 500 years before he lived there had been a Golden Age. During this time people lived together in peace and harmony. Their way of life provided an example of how to live properly. [*See also* EAST ASIA; TAOISM.]

CONGREGATION ✴ A group of people, most often Jewish or Christian, gathered together for religious WORSHIP. The word can also refer to all of the members of a particular local CHURCH or SYNAGOGUE. In the BIBLE the word often refers to the entire Israelite community or to a simple gathering of several people. In ROMAN CATHOLICISM, there are several formal congregations, such as the College of Cardinals who meet to elect a new POPE.

CONVERSION ❧ The process of changing from one religion to another. Conversion is a personal decision. It may happen as the result of the work of a MISSIONARY. Often, when people decide to convert to another religion, they go to classes to learn the traditions and beliefs of the new religion. For example, Jewish converts learn about JUDAISM in a year-long course taught by a rabbi. Converts also usually participate in ceremonies to become full members of their new FAITH.

CREATION ❧ The act of bringing the universe into being. Each religion has its own beliefs about how the world was made. For example, the first book of the BIBLE describes how God created the world, according to followers of JUDAISM and CHRISTIANITY. Certain Pacific Ocean societies believe that the earth and the sky are the parents of everything that exists. Certain cultures in India hold that the world was created from an egg. The egg's lower half is the earth, and the top half is the sky. All other things in the universe are made from the inside of the egg. [*See also* EVOLUTION.]

CROSS ❧ A SYMBOL in which two lines intersect, or cross, each other. In CHRISTIANITY the cross is a symbol of Jesus Christ, who was nailed

Easter

Followers of CHRISTIANITY celebrate Easter to remember that Jesus Christ rose from the dead to conquer SIN. It is celebrated on the Sunday after the first full moon after March 21. Good Friday, the Friday before Easter Sunday, is remembered as the day Jesus died on a CROSS. Christians believe Easter Sunday is the day of Jesus' resurrection, or rising from the dead. It is the most important holiday of the Christian year.

Easter may have gotten its name from the Northern European GODDESS of spring, Eostre. Today, Easter is celebrated by a visit from the Easter rabbit and by dying Easter eggs. Both are SYMBOLS of spring. Special FOODS, such as hot-cross buns, are part of Easter. Also, Christians traditionally wear new, spring clothing to their religious service on Easter Sunday.

to a cross to die. A cross may be bare, or it may show Jesus Christ suffering—a crucifix. Crosses are found in many religious settings, such as in CHURCHES, in artwork, in homes, and on jewelry.

D

DALAI LAMA ☙ A Buddhist monk and spiritual leader of Tibetan BUDDHISM. He was also the ruler of Tibet, until he fled the country after a 1959 revolution. Today, the Dalai Lama lives in India. He travels the world explaining BUDDHISM and working for world peace and cooperation among religions. In 1989 he received the Nobel Peace Prize. Each Dalai Lama is identified from among a number of young boys born shortly after the death of the previous Dalai Lama. The child who reaches out to touch certain religious things actually used by the previous one, instead of reaching for imitations, is then raised as the new Dalai Lama. [*See also* MONKS AND NUNS.]

The Dalai Lama spreads his message of tolerance around the world.

DANCE ☙ A central part of WORSHIP and religious experience in many religions. In tribal societies, everyone may take part in dances to thank the GODS for a successful hunt or harvest. Sometimes, as in SHINTO and HINDUISM, specially trained artists may perform beautiful dances as an offering to honor and entertain the gods. They may also act out a sacred MYTH to help people remember its story. In mystical groups like the SUFIS of ISLAM, whirling dances help persons go into religious TRANCE or ecstasy. Sometimes in PENTECOSTAL Christian services, worshipers may freely begin dancing to express their religious joy.

DEATH ☙ The condition of a body that no longer has life. Also, the moment when this condition begins. In most religions, death is thought of as the departure of the SOUL from its body. The soul is usually believed to go to a place of reward or punishment. Some religions teach that the

The Day of the Dead is celebrated throughout Mexico.

Day of the Dead

All Souls Day, November 2, as celebrated in Mexico. In the early Middle Ages, Christians began to believe that they should honor all of the dead, and not just the saints, on a special day. The day chosen for this was the day after All Saints Day, which came to be known as All Souls Day. On All Souls Day in Mexico, people carry food, flowers, toys, gifts, and religious objects to their cemeteries. There they have an outdoor meal, and rejoice with all of the dead in heaven, especially those whose bodies are buried in the cemetery in which they have gathered. Children especially enjoy this day, and they play and sing with their families.

soul is reborn into another body after death. Religions usually hold FUNERALS, to help the departed person in the next world with prayers or offerings. Funerals also help the people who are still living mourn their loss. In some religions, such as HINDUISM, the corpse is burned, and its smoke rises to the sky as a sign of a new life. [*See also* AFTERLIFE; REBIRTH; REINCARNATION.]

DEMONS ✵ Evil spirits that can cause SIN and SUFFERING in human lives. Some people believe that a demon can control everything a person thinks and does. In that case, the person is said to be "possessed" by the demon. Many religions have a strong tradition of the reality of demons. In Hinduism, for example, demons are spirits that work against the gods. JUDAISM, CHRISTIANITY, and ISLAM also have such traditions. When a person becomes "possessed" by a demon, often the only hope is for the demon be driven out ("exorcised") by someone of special holiness or authority. In modern times, belief in demons has become less common. [*See also* SATAN.]

DENOMINATIONS ✵ An organized group of churches that is part of a larger religious faith. For example, METHODISTS, BAPTISTS, and Lutherans are three of the many de-

Halloween

The evening of October 31. The name HALLOWEEN comes from "All Hallows' Eve," the day before All Saints Day in CHRISTIANITY. On Halloween, GHOSTS and DEMONS are supposed to roam about, doing mischief. Halloween is thought to have originated with the DRUIDS, who believed that evil spirits were released to the earth on October 31. Today, Halloween is usually celebrated by children in ghostly or fanciful costumes who go from door to door to ask for a "treat" in exchange for the understanding that they will do no "trick" or mischief.

nominations of PROTESTANTISM. Each denomination has its own way of worshiping. Each also has its own ministers and its own churches. Certain types of BUDDHISM, such as Zen Buddhism, can be considered denominations because they have their own devotional practices and beliefs.

DEVOTION ❧ A religious act or feeling that shows a strong commitment to God. A religious person or group of people might show devotion by bowing toward religious symbols, kneeling in prayer, or just having deep inner feelings of reverence toward the sacred. The earliest Buddhists showed devotion by prostration, or lying flat on the ground in PRAYER. People who make PILGRIMAGES perform certain acts of devotion. But for many people, devotion is simply a matter of regular prayer and inward attachment toward God.

DISCIPLES ❧ Followers of a teacher or of a way of life. In the NEW TESTAMENT a disciple was any follower of Jesus Christ. However, the word usually refers to the 12 APOSTLES, or close followers, of Jesus Christ. Today, a disciple can be a follower of any religion or school of thought. [See also APOSTLES.]

DIVINATION ❧ See PROPHETS.

DOCTRINE ❧ The official set of teachings of a religion. Religious doctrine keeps a religion's practices the same over time. It also helps the religion's leaders decide if a person or practice is in error, or against the beliefs of the faith. Church doctrine also serves as a religious authority, much like the laws of a nation. For example, church doctine would explain when and how the faith's ceremonies should be performed.

DOGMA ❧ See DOCTRINE.

DRAMA ✣ A play that tells a story and shows something important about life. Religious drama may simply be the acting out of an important event, such as the founding of the faith. Religious drama may also be intended to show the spirit world, as when actors play the part of ANGELS or DEMONS. In Japan, drama is often based on the religion of ZEN BUDDHISM. In China, drama is often used to teach the religious values of goodness and loyalty. In ISLAM, stick puppets are used to cast shadows on a sheet for a play about common sense. [*See also* FOUNDERS; SPIRIT.]

DRUIDS ✣ The priests, prophets, and other leaders of Druidism, a Celtic religion that appeared in France, Britain, and Ireland about the second century B.C.E. Druids had a great respect for nature, especially oaks and mistletoe. They worshiped in oak forests. Certain stone structures still found in their regions are thought to have been their altars. Druids believed in astrology and magic. They considered the soul immortal, since at death it always entered the body of a newborn infant. The Romans destroyed Druidism in regions they controlled. Druidism then continued only in isolated parts of Britain and Ireland until the coming of CHRISTIANITY. [*See also* ALTAR; NATURE; PRIEST; SOUL.]

Stonehenge, in England, may have been a holy site for the Druids.

DRUMS ✣ A percussion instrument that comes in different shapes and sizes, struck with sticks or the hands. Drums are used in religious ceremonies all over the world. For example, SHAMANS may use drums to communicate with SPIRITS. The sound transports the shaman into the realm of the spirits. Africans have made particular use of the drum in religious WORSHIP. Today, people of African descent in the Caribbean and NORTH AMERICA continue to use the drum in worship. [*See also* AFRICAN AMERICAN RELIGIONS; NATIVE AMERICAN RELIGIONS.]

Ashanti ceremonial drummers

EARTH ❧ The planet on which we live and an important part of the religious tradition of many cultures. Creation stories from all over the world center on the divine beginning of the Earth. The Babylonians believed that the Earth was created from the body of the great sea monster, Tiamat. Native Americans are especially known to revere the Earth because they see the Earth as source of all life. [*See also* CIVILIZATIONS, ANCIENT; NATIVE AMERICAN RELIGIONS.]

EAST ASIA ❧ East Asia includes the countries of China, Japan, and Korea. Several religions began in East Asia. CONFUCIANISM and TAOISM began in China. SHINTO began in Japan.

In ancient times, MISSIONARIES from INDIA brought BUDDHISM to China. From there it spread to Korea and Japan. Starting in the 1500s, missionaries from EUROPE and then NORTH AMERICA brought CHRISTIANITY to East Asia. It is now especially strong in Korea.

People in East Asia often practice more than one religion. They do not see the need to choose just one religion, as people in North America usually do. Japanese have traditionally practiced both Buddhism and Shinto, while Chinese have traditionally practiced Confucianism, Taoism, and Buddhism, plus what some people call folk religion. Folk religion includes common practices, like giving OFFERINGS to a local goddess in order to have a child. Folk religions are based on traditional practices and do not have written scriptures.

When the Communists started to rule China in 1949, they discouraged people from being religious altogether. Nevertheless, religions have made big contributions to East Asian culture.

Health and Medicine. People in East Asia have traditionally used several special techniques to keep their bodies healthy and to promote healing. Slow-motion exercises like Tai Chi and martial arts, such as Aikido, keep the body in good shape. Acupuncture, which comes from China, uses needles to relieve pain. Martial arts and other physical exercises sometimes put the ideas of

Taoism and Buddhism into practice. Physical exercises and healing arts try to bring about this harmony.

Ethics and Family Life. Confucianism has had an important influence on ethics and family life in East Asia. Confucius taught that one of the most important virtues was "reciprocity." To explain what this means, he taught the golden rule: "Do not do to anyone what you would not want them to do to you." He also taught that everyone who wants to live the right kind of life should start by respecting their parents. As a result, the Confucian virtue known as *hsiao*; or "respect for one's parents," has been very important. It does not apply only to children. It guides adults as they care for elderly parents who need special care. This respect also shows in the traditional practice of giving offerings to ancestors.

Art and Architecture. Taoism and Zen Buddhism have guided artists and architects in East Asia. Both religions teach people to look to nature for divine inspiration. Some Chinese and Japanese artists have painted landscapes that try to convey this experience. In an unusual kind of landscape painting inspired by Zen, the artist throws ink at the paper. The shapes that result may suggest a landscape. In this way, the artist tries to show people the Zen Buddhist teaching that the mind constructs a world from the impressions of the senses.

Zen Meditation

The word *zen* comes from a word that means meditation. It refers to a kind of BUDDHISM that emphasizes meditation.

The most common form of Zen meditation is called *zazen*, seated meditation. Many Zen meditators sit on a firm, round pillow called a *zafu*. Another kind of Zen meditation takes place while walking.

When meditating, Zen Buddhists try to reach a state of mind that they call *satori*. Actually, they say *satori* is a state of "no mind," but no one can reach it by trying. They try to reach this state in two different ways. Members of the Rinzai school work on riddles, called *koan*, that their teachers have given them. Members of the Soto school see just sitting, without thinking about anything, as the best approach.

Some Zen teachers say that Zen meditation can help people no matter what religion they are. In the United States, some adults have started to do Zen meditation for help with problems like stress. Children may do meditation similar to Zen in martial arts classes.

Chinese and Japanese gardens reflect the Taoist and Zen emphasis on nature, too. Gardens like those at

Suzhou, China, create little bits of nature in the middle of a busy city. Some Japanese gardens inspired by Zen, such as the garden at Ryoanji in Kyoto, do not use water at all. They use small stones and rocks, which may be raked in such a way as to suggest waves. These "dry gardens" provide a place to do Zen meditation. [*See also* NEW RELIGIOUS MOVEMENTS.]

EASTERN ORTHODOXY

See ORTHODOXY, EASTERN.

EDUCATION, RELIGIOUS

The training of people in religious beliefs and the religious life. All religions educate children and other newcomers to their faith. In close-knit traditional societies, religious training may be done in the home. In countries with an official religion, religious education may be part of regular schooling, along with subjects like social studies and math. [In other countries, such as the United States which practices the separation of church and state, religious education must be done either in private schools or in special classes like Sunday school or Hebrew school.] Religions also usually provide special training for leaders like PRIESTS, MONKS, and NUNS. [*See also* TEACHERS.]

END OF THE WORLD

A time when the world as we know it will end. Each religion has different beliefs about what will happen at that time. The book of Revelation in the NEW TESTAMENT tells the Christian belief about the end of the world. It describes a war in which the armies of HEAVEN overcome the armies of SATAN. Most religious people do not think this story is literally true. Many believe that it simply tells how GOOD will defeat EVIL. Other religions, such as ISLAM, believe that a MESSIAH, or savior, will come at the end of the world. For HINDUISM and BUDDHISM, the end of the world is when creatures will find enlightenment in their cycle of REBIRTH.

ETERNITY

The idea of unending time or a state of being beyond all time. Eternity is often used to mean days without end in the AFTERLIFE in HEAVEN or HELL. In religious study, eternity also refers to the state of GOD, NIRVANA, or other unending reality. [*See also* DEATH; FUNERALS.]

ETHICS

The study of right and wrong behavior. Religious ethics judge behavior according to important principles of a faith, such as the TEN COMMANDMENTS. In HINDUISM and BUDDHISM, an important ethical belief is that right or wrong behavior in the present life will cause good or bad things to happen in a future life. [*See also* AFTERLIFE; BIBLE; KARMA; REINCARNATION.]

EUROPE ❧ Europe—a continent that stretches north from the Mediterranean Sea and east from the Atlantic Ocean to Russia—is where some of the most important forms of CHRISTIANITY and JUDAISM arose.

During the 300s C.E. Christianity became the official religion of the Roman Empire. From there it spread north to the rest of Europe. Eventually it became the official religion of almost every country in Europe.

In 1054 the Orthodox churches in eastern Europe and the Catholic church in the rest of Europe split apart. They did so because of differences in language, culture, and politics as well as religious belief and practice. Then in the 1500s Protestants left the Catholic church in a movement they called the Reformation. They first did so in response to the teachings of Martin Luther. These forms of Christianity created distinctive styles of worship, architecture, art, and music.

By the Middle Ages, Jews had also settled in Spain, Germany, and eastern Europe. Spanish or "Sephardic" Jews developed a different culture and tradition of worship from those of the Ashkenazic Jews in Germany and eastern Europe. At the end of the 1400s, Christians drove the Jews out of Spain, but important Jewish communities continued to exist in central and eastern Europe until the mid-1900s. In the 1700s, Hasidic Jews in eastern Europe formed communities around righteous teachers. During the 1800s, some Jewish groups in Germany tried to "update" Judaism, by bringing in certain Christian traditions, such as choirs that sang during services.

A small number of MUSLIMS have lived in Europe for centuries. Today, Muslims are moving into Europe in greater numbers. Their presence is making European religions and cultures even more diverse.

Styles of Worship. Orthodox, Catholic, and Protestant Christians have different styles of worship. Orthodox and Catholic worship centers on the celebration of a RITUAL called the Eucharist, Communion, or the Lord's Supper. This ritual recalls Jesus' last meal with his disciples.

Protestants also celebrate the Lord's Supper, but usually less often.

St. Peter's Cathedral in Rome is the center of Roman Catholicism.

Their worship centers on reading from the BIBLE and a SERMON, a talk in which a minister or other qualified person explains the Bible. Protestants have also emphasized singing HYMNS together. At the time of the Reformation, the strictest Protestants only allowed psalms from the Bible to be sung.

Architecture. Until the 1700s, the history of European architecture was mostly the history of religious buildings. The Gothic-style church is a very popular style of church building. It arose in Europe about 1,000 years ago. Gothic churches were the first churches to use stained-glass windows. On the outside they have tall arches, called flying buttresses, that support the walls. A famous Gothic church is the cathedral at Chartres, France.

Art. Worship in Orthodox churches is especially known for its use of pictures called ICONS. They are an important European tradition of religious art.

In the Middle Ages, Catholic artists crafted many items for churches and worship services. These include stained-glass windows, statues, paintings, and plates and cups for celebrating the Eucharist. Many Protestants rejected the use of artwork; they thought it was idolatry—the worshiping of IMAGES instead of God. But the

Catholic church continued to encourage artwork. Some of the most famous European works of art, such as "The Last Supper" by Leonardo da Vinci, decorate churches.

For most of history Jews have been much more interested in writing than in architecture and art. But there have been notable exceptions, such as the Russian Jewish artist, Marc Chagall (1887–1985), who often created religious works of art.

Music. European religious music began with Gregorian chants—melodies sung by priests and CHOIRS during worship in the Middle Ages. Beginning with the Reformation, Protestants have written hymns for congregations to sing during worship. As European music developed, Christianity provided the themes and occasions for well-known musical pieces. One example is "The Messiah" by Georg Friedrich Handel, with its famous "Hallelujah Chorus."

In Jewish tradition, singers known as cantors have led worship services. As a result, European Judaism developed rich traditions of music to use in worship. An example is the song "Kol Nidre."

EVANGELICALISM ❧ In the English-speaking world, a type of PROTESTANTISM that began as a movement in the METHODIST church. Followers of Evangelicalism go

Evangelical protestants are filled with the Holy Spirit at a revival meeting.

through a deep, personal CONVERSION experience. They believe that this experience brings them God's grace. After conversion, each person tries to live a completely pure, holy, and sinless life. This conversion experience is the reason they are sometimes called "born again Christians." Evangelicals believe that the Holy Spirit, a member of the TRINITY, brings God's blessing. Evangelicals often hold revival meetings where people renew their deep faith. They send many MISSIONARIES to teach their religion. They also believe that it is wrong to drink alcohol.

EVIL ✤ The force or power that brings about bad things. Some religions, such as CHRISTIAN SCIENCE and some types of HINDUISM, believe that evil does not exist—that it is only in our minds. Many followers of CHRISTIANITY, JUDAISM, and ISLAM believe that evil is a punishment that humans deserve for disobeying God. Members of some Eastern religions believe that evil comes from a person's KARMA, which is the cause and effect chain of thoughts, words, and actions. [*See also* ETHICS; SNAKE.]

EVOLUTION ✤ A theory about how life began on EARTH. The theory is supported by the work of Charles Darwin (1809–1882). His studies showed how simple life forms could have evolved into more complicated ones through a process called *natural selection*. Some people believe evolution is opposed to the religious ideas of creation. But others say that God could have worked through evolution.

EXPERIENCE, RELIGIOUS ✤ A strong joyous or awesome inner feeling that religious people take to mean God is present in them or is with them. People may feel thankful for good things God has given them and for PRAYERS that have been answered. They may just feel a deep love for God. In other instances, they may feel sorry for SIN and feel the cleansing power of God's forgiveness in religious experience.

F G

FAITH ✵ Belief in something that cannot or does not need to be proven, as in, "faith in God." Faith can also be used as another word for *religion*, as in, "the Christian faith."

FAMILY ✵ The most basic group of human society. A family is made up of one or two parents or guardians and the children they bring up. It is in the family that people usually first learn their religious beliefs and practices. Many religions include the family at the center of much of their worship and other activities. In JUDAISM, for example, the Passover supper is a family celebration of the most important event in Hebrew history, the liberation of the people from slavery. [*See also* HOME, RELIGION IN; RITUAL.]

FARMING SOCIETIES ✵ People first discovered how to grow food in the MIDDLE EAST about 12,000 years ago. Soon religions were taking agriculture very seriously.

One of the oldest farming societies arose at Çatalhöyük, Turkey, about 8,500 years ago. Some people claim that these farmers worshiped a GODDESS who helped their fields produce FOOD.

Later, many people in the Middle East told stories about a goddess who spent part of the year on earth and part of the year under it. The Greeks called this goddess Persephone, and many people connect her with plants like wheat.

Religion often addresses problems that farmers face. The Hopi live in northeastern Arizona where it is dry. They perform ceremonies to make sure rain comes. In the ceremonies masked male dancers called *kachinas* play the roles of the spirits who first brought rain.

FASTING ✵ A time when a person does not eat or drink, often for religious reasons. For example, members of JUDAISM fast for one full day on *Yom Kippur*, or the Day of Atonement. They do this as a way to repent their SINS and to ask forgiveness from God. Certain Native American groups fast to help them bring on spiritual visions. Some people fast as a way to make their bodies pure. Fasting can be a time when

Lent

Some people who practice CHRISTI-ANITY celebrate Lent during the 40 days before EASTER. It is a time of FASTING that recalls when Jesus fasted in the wilderness. The day before Lent begins is a festival day called Shrove Tuesday, Pancake Day, or MARDI GRAS. It is a time to use the FOOD, such as eggs and fat, that traditionally cannot be eaten during the Lenten fast. The first day of Lent is called Ash Wednesday, when some Christians are marked with ashes on their foreheads. In this way they show sorrow for their SINS. The last week of Lent is called Holy Week. It begins with Palm Sunday. On this day, Christians remember the palms that the people used as they greeted Jesus when he entered Jerusalem. The Friday of Holy Week is called Good Friday. It is remembered as the day Jesus was crucified.

only certain FOODS are restricted (such as meat for Christians on Fridays during Lent) or when foods are restricted at certain times. For example, followers of ISLAM fast in the daytime during the month of Ramadan. They only eat one meal after dark and a light meal before dawn.

FESTIVALS ✧ Public celebrations, usually accompanied by the serving of FOOD and drink ("feasting") and by expressions of joy. Traditionally, religious festivals are held at a particular time of the year to honor a holy person, place, thing, or time of year. Religious festivals often show the joy that people have in their religious beliefs and practices. The traditions of festivals sometimes come down from ancient times. Examples of ancient and joyous religious festivals are the Tibetan or Chinese New Year. [*See also* HOLIDAYS; LIGHT (HANUKKAH); NEW YEAR'S CELEBRATION; TIBET.]

A procession during a traditional Japanese festival

FIRE ✧ A powerful religious SYMBOL. In many Christian churches, the fire of candlelight shows the purity of God and spiritual things. Fire also speaks of the energy of God, as when, according to the NEW TESTA-

MENT, the Holy Spirit came as tongues of fire to the apostles at Pentecost. Fire out of control, however, brings suffering and destruction. Religiously, this side of fire shows that evil must be punished and burned away, as by the traditional fires of HELL. In HINDUISM, the fire god, Agni, is the god who receives sacrifices. In ZOROASTRIANISM, a fire is kept perpetually burning in temples to symbolize God's presence. In several faiths, candles are lit during services to symbolize the holiness of the ceremony. [*See also* LIGHT.]

FISH ✳ A very old SYMBOL for Jesus Christ. In Greek, the letters that begin the words *Jesus Christ, Son of God, Savior* spell out the word *fish*. The fish symbol took on greater meaning in CHRISTIANITY since MISSIONARIES are sometimes called "fishers of men."

FLOOD ✳ The complete covering of the EARTH with water, part of the sacred history of many religions. Native Americans in the Northwest Coast cultures believe that a flood took place during the first days of the Earth. Flood stories are often related to destruction and punishment. The Aztecs believed that a flood, lasting 52 years, once destroyed the world. In the BIBLE God punished people for their SINS by calling for rain for 40 days and 40 nights.

FOLK RELIGION ✳ Religious ideas and practices based on custom and tradition. Many religions contain some elements of a folk religion. For example, belief in Halloween ghosts is part of ancient folk religion. [*See also* DEMONS; DRUIDS; GODS; MIRACLES; OCCULTISM; POLYTHEISM; SPIRIT; TABOO; VOODOO; WITCHCRAFT.]

FOOD ✳ An important part of many religions' rules. Sometimes food is restricted on days of FASTING such as during Lent for many members of CHRISTIANITY. On other days, special foods are eaten. For example, in ISLAM, dates and water are eaten at the end of each day during the month of Ramadan. Sometimes special food is eaten at certain times of the year. For example, Jews eat a special bread called *Challah* on the holiday Purim. In some religions, certain foods are not permitted at all. For example,

Traditional foods are an important part of the Jewish Passover celebration.

Passover

A holiday that commemorates freedom for members of JUDAISM. It is celebrated for eight days in March or April. The holiday recalls an event called the Exodus when Jews escaped from slavery in Egypt. During Passover, Jews celebrate a special meal called the *seder*. During the seder, a disk holds special foods that are SYMBOLS of events in Jewish history. For example, salt water recalls tears, bitter herbs recall the bitterness of slavery, and special bread, Matzo, recalls the hurried escape from Egypt. Each FOOD helps tell the story of the Exodus. There is a special custom at every seder dinner to set a place at the table for the PROPHET Elijah. It is said that one day he will come down from HEAVEN with great news.

members of Islam do not eat pork. Some religions have complicated rules about food. The kosher diet for observant Jews has rules about which meats and fish are permitted and how foods should be prepared.

FOOLS ✴ Individuals who perform silly or funny acts. In religions, fools are sometimes RITUAL CLOWNS who bring HUMOR to religious services.

FOUNDERS ✴ Those who began the great religions. People like the Buddha, Jesus, or Muhammad are the founders or original teachers of some of the major religions. They have had a tremendous impact on history, which is felt to this day.

FREEDOM, RELIGIOUS ✴ The right to practice the religion of one's choice. In many traditional societies, everyone practiced the same religion. People who lived together had the same ideas and worshipped in the same way. In modern times, many people have become tolerant of others' faiths. In addition, many people have come to believe that government should be separate from religion. Thus democracy, freedom of religion, and its separation from government control is guaranteed in the United States and other modern countries. Lack of real religious freedom is still found in some places, however.

FREE WILL ✴ The ability to make choices that are not determined by someone else or by God. Members of some DENOMINATIONS, such as CALVINISM, believe that people do not have complete free will. Calvinists hold that the choice people make for faith in Christ has already been decided by God. Other traditions hold that humans are free to choose good or evil deeds. They hold that each person, not God, is responsible for his or her own actions. Many people argue that a person can be thought of as good only if they have the free will to be evil.

FUNDAMENTALISM ❧ A movement of PROTESTANTISM similar to EVANGELICALISM. It began around the 1920s and 1930s. Christians who have fundamentalist views believe that the words of the BIBLE are literally true. They do not believe in EVOLUTION. Also, they believe that other types of CHRISTIANITY are false. Today, leaders of the fundamentalist movement are very active in politics in some parts of the United States. [*See also* EVANGELICALISM.]

FUNERALS ❧ A special ceremony held after a person dies. Each religious TRADITION has different RITUALS for funerals. Some religions believe that a dead person will need supplies for their journey after death. For example, in Chinese religions, items such as FOOD, flowers, or paper goods are buried with the dead person for use in the next world. Members of other religions bury weapons or coins to help pay the cost of the journey. Some religions, such as JUDAISM and ISLAM, prepare a body for burial by cleaning it and wrapping it in special cloths. Members of some religions believe that a body should be buried facing a

Funeral rites are a part of most religious traditions.

certain direction. Muslims face the body toward MECCA. Japanese Buddhists face the body's head toward the north. Some funerals for members of Christian religions are very elaborate. They can include a long procession of people following a casket. In Judaism, a FAMILY often observes deep mourning for seven days after burying a loved one.

GAMES AND PLAY ❧ Human activities that are enjoyable and sometimes competitive. The roots of games and religious RITUAL probably come from the same source in ancient human culture—the need to stop day-to-day work and express human feelings and emotions. In religion, people break from their everyday work to express their beliefs in their God or GODS through worship, which may include DANCE and song, as well as PRAYER. Similarly, games and play include joyful expressions. The Olympic games of ancient Greece began with sacrifices to the gods. In Japan, tugs-of-war, horse racing, and other games can be traced back to ancient Shinto rituals. Tournaments in the Middle Ages began with the Catholic Mass.

Today, many athletes find that meditation or the state of keen awareness as taught by Zen BUDDHISM help them in their competition. It may help by focusing the athletes' energy and attention on the game.

GODDESSES ✤ Female deities in polytheistic religions. For example, Isis was a goddess in ancient Egypt. She was the goddess of fertility, the ability to create life. Hera and Athena are goddesses in the ancient Greek religion. Athena is the goddess of wisdom and war. Hera is the goddess of women and marriage. Goddesses are most often connected to the EARTH, love, and the HARVEST. [See also POLYTHEISM.]

GODS ✤ Male deities in polytheistic religions. Gods are often associated with the sky, war, kingship, and fertility. For example, in Norse mythology, Thor is god of thunder, war, and strength. The god Odin, sometimes called Woden, is the Norse god of art, culture, war, and the dead. Osirus is an Egyptian god who is lord of the underworld. Zeus, in ancient Greek religion, is king of the gods. [See also POLYTHEISM.]

GOOD ✤ The quality of being moral, righteous, or virtuous. Many religions teach that God is perfectly good and that all good things in the world come from God. Members of other religions, such as HINDUISM and BUDDHISM, feel that humans bring on good things and evil things through their own personal KARMA. [See also ETHICS; EVIL.]

GURU ✤ A personal spiritual guide. Gurus have been important throughout Hindu history. For example, most of the persons who practice *bhakti*, one of the great Hindu paths to religious perfection, claim that their beliefs have been handed down by holy gurus from prehistoric times. This unbroken line guarantess them the correctness of their beliefs and practices. The practice of meeting with a guru has also spread to some non-Hindu groups. [See also HINDUISM; MYSTICISM; SCRIPTURES.]

H

HARVEST ❧ The reaping or gathering of ripened grain, vegetables, or fruit. Traditionally, the harvest was done by all the men, women, and older children of the community. Since prehistoric times, this labor has been accompanied by acts of thanksgiving to God or to the GODS, and by joyful celebrations. Examples of harvest festivals are the African American Kwanzaa; the Jewish Sukkot; and the Protestant Christian Thanksgiving, first celebrated in 1621—the forerunner of the national Thanksgiving Day in the United States. [*See also* AFRICAN AMERICAN RELIGIONS; FESTIVALS; HOLIDAYS; JUDAISM; PROTESTANTISM.]

HEALING ❧ The belief that SICKNESS can be cured by religious means. For example, SHAMANS in tribal societies were believed able to drive out EVIL spirits and restore health. Shamans danced and chanted as they tried to drive the sickness, and the DEMON that caused it, from the ill person. In CHRISTIANITY, some people believe that the laying on of

Thanksgiving

In the year 1621, the governor of Plymouth Colony proclaimed a day of thanksgiving to God for the especially fine harvest that had been reaped that year. Joined by neighboring Native Americans, the Pilgrims feasted and gave thanks. This was the first Thanksgiving Day. The custom gradually spread, at first in New England, and then to many states across the United States.

In 1863, President Abraham Lincoln proclaimed a Day of Thanksgiving for the entire country. Every President since then has issued a Thanksgiving Proclamation. Thanksgiving Day in the United States now falls on the fourth Thursday of November. In Canada, Thanksgiving Day is the second Monday of October. A turkey dinner is customary in many families during their celebration of this day.

Oral Roberts, performing a healing by the laying on of hands

hands with PRAYER can impart God's healing power. Sacred shrines, such as Lourdes in France, are famous for spiritual healing. People go on PILGRIMAGES to be healed. Many people also believe that prayer and meditation can help the sick find the energy to fight disease.

HEAVEN ✤ The place where God dwells. Each religion has a different idea about where heaven is, who lives there, and who goes there. In some religions, heaven is the place above the earth where God lives and where humans may go after they die. On judgment day, God decides who has lived a virtuous life on EARTH and might be worthy of entering heaven. Some other religions, such as HINDUISM, teach that heaven is the place where people who have had very good KARMA are reborn after they die. Some religious books have described heaven. The BIBLE describes it as a jeweled city. The QU'RAN describes it as a garden with flowing rivers and green plants. Heaven always symbolizes the beauty and splendor of God.

HELL ✤ The place where SATAN lives. In some religions, it is the place under the earth where wicked people go as punishment after they die. In most religions, it is a place of torture. Hell is often described as a fiery place where sinners burn. Sometimes hell is described as icy cold. Some Islamic and Christian writers have thought that a person might be able to get out of hell through virtue and penitence, or sorrow for their wickedness. Members of HINDUISM and BUDDHISM think of hell as one of the places where very bad sinners might be reborn.

HERDING SOCIETIES ✤ In herding societies, people live by looking after flocks or herds of animals. The ancient Israelites, ancestors of the Jews, were an ancient herding society. Abraham, Isaac, and Jacob had donkeys and flocks of sheep. More recent herders include the Nuer in eastern Africa, who herd

Because the ancient Jews were herders, the parable of the lost sheep was easy to understand.

cattle and the Sami in the far north of Europe, who herd reindeer.

Most herders are nomads. They travel from place to place with their flocks. Nomadic herders have religious practices that fit their ways of life.

The ancient Israelites knew a God connected to a particular family, "the God of Abraham, Isaac, and Jacob." Members of the FAMILY could worship this God wherever they went. The Nuer worship a "high god," a spirit who is everywhere, whom they call Kwoth Nhial. The Sami are now Christian, but in the past they seem to have made OFFERINGS at different spots that they would pass as they wandered with their herds.

HERMIT ❧

A religious person who chooses to live a solitary life of WORSHIP. Hermits feel that they can worship God more purely if they are alone and away from society. In the early days of CHRISTIANITY, hermits were thought to be filled with HOLINESS. People made special trips to ask the advice of certain hermits. Today, the word *hermit* can refer to any person who lives a solitary life away from society.

HEROES AND HEROINES ❧

Great men and women and their stories. Heroic figures in MYTHS thrill us with their strength and daring. For example, Hercules of ancient Greece killed a nine-headed monster and brought back golden apples. Religious figures like the SAINTS and FOUNDERS of the great religions are also heroes and heroines. They fight DEMONS and bring SALVATION, though only after suffering. The Buddha fasted and meditated a long time to gain enlightenment, though the demon Mara tried to make him give up. According to CHRISTIANITY, Jesus, after FASTING in the desert, rejected Satan's temptation to turn stones into bread. Jesus also rejected Satan's offer to become ruler of the world. Then, Jesus suffered on the cross to bring salvation to humanity. Heroes and heroines inspire people because they have a human side, yet do deeds worthy of the GODS.

HINDUISM ☙

Hinduism is the ancient religion of the subcontinent of India. It is also the dominant religion of the area.

Most Hindus live in India, but Hindus also live in other places, including the United States and CANADA.

Beliefs. Hindus have different beliefs about God. Some Hindus worship many GODS. Some worship one god. Some do not believe in God at all.

The most popular gods that Hindus worship are Shiva, the god also known as Siva, and Vishnu. Vishnu has appeared on EARTH in many forms, such as Rama and Krishna, to save the world from evil. The fat belly and the elephant head of another popular god, Ganesha, make him easy to recognize. He is the god of all beginnings.

Most Hindus believe that after people die, they are born again. But Hindus also believe that people will die again, even if they have been reborn in HEAVEN. Hindus call the continuing cycle of being born and dying *samsara*.

A Hindu holy man, known as a *sadh*, meditates.

What a person does in life—*karma*—determines where a person will be reborn next and as what. If a person does good deeds, that person's next life will be good. Some Hindus strive to achieve *moksha*, an "escape" from rebirth altogether.

Practices. Most Hindus do a form of worship called *puja*. They present OFFERINGS before IMAGES of gods, they gaze upon the images as if they were looking upon the gods themselves, and they receive some offerings, known as *prasada*, back from the gods. Hindus often perform *puja* at home, but they can also do it in a TEMPLE.

Some Hindus perform very old rituals, called "Vedic rituals." These rituals involve giving SACRIFICES. Ancient Indians sacrificed animals, but today people simply sacrifice plant products, such as grain. Hindus may also practice YOGA. Some do so to achieve *moksha*, or escape from rebirth.

Hindus celebrate many festivals. Diwali, the festival of lights, marks the new year. Like Rosh Hashanah, the Jewish New Year, it takes place in the fall. In the spring, Holi is a time for fun.

Social Institutions. By tradition, Hindus are born into castes (*jatis*), just as they are born into families. The brahmin (priest) castes are the purest ones, followed by *kshatriya* (warrior), *vaishya* (merchant), and *shudra* (servant) castes. The Dalits, formerly called untouchables, are supposedly the most impure of all.

Hindus traditionally believe that people should perform certain rituals, including marriage, only with members of their caste. Therefore, traditional Hindus marry someone who belongs to the same caste.

In India today, especially in big cities, castes are less important than they used to be. It is illegal today to discriminate against people because of their caste, although this law is hard to enforce. In addition, the government of India has a strict quota system. It reserves more than 25 percent of all places in schools, universities, and government offices for people of the lowest castes.

Ethics and Ideals. Hindu scriptures recognize four goals in life. These are to have pleasure (*kama*),

The Life of Krishna

Krishna, whose name means "black" or "dark blue," is one of the most popular GODS of Hinduism. Some Hindus, such as the "Hare Krishnas," worship Krishna as the Supreme God, but most consider him a form of the god Vishnu. They say that Vishnu came to EARTH as Krishna to preserve *dharma* and defeat EVIL.

Hindus tell many stories about Krishna on Earth. In some stories he is a handsome, fun-loving young man who enchants young women (the *gopis*, or "cow-herding girls") and plays pranks on them. Hindus believe that these stories actually teach how God plays with the world (*lila*) and enchants the human SOUL.

As an adult, Krishna discusses life, rebirth, *dharma*, and similar topics with his close friend, the warrior Arjuna. These conversations make up the BHAGAVAD GITA.

Because Hindus hold Krishna in such reverence, Indian artists frequently depict him. They usually show him with dark blue skin, and he is often playing a flute. At other times he is sitting or standing with his consort, Radha—a common image in Krishna temples.

to gain wealth (*artha*), to act properly (*dharma*), and to escape from rebirth (*moksha*). Hindus believe that it is good to seek pleasure and wealth, as long as one follows the rules of *dharma* to get them. These rules also prescribe what people of different ages and castes should do. For example, young people should study. Their parents should work, traditionally in a job suited to their caste, have families, and perform the family's worship.

HOLIDAYS ✵ Days on which custom requires a pause in ordinary business. Holidays usually fall on particular days of the week or year. Holidays may be either religious or nonreligious. FESTIVALS are often celebrated on holidays. Religious holidays are special times of PRAYER and RITUAL. Examples of religious holidays are the Jewish Passover; the weekly Christian Lord's Day (Sunday); the Muslim Hajj, or PILGRIMAGE to MECCA; the Chinese Birthday of the Lotus; and the Nigerian New Yam Festival. [*See also* AFRICA; CHRISTIANITY; ISLAM; JUDAISM.]

HOLINESS ✵ A sacred, divine, or ultimate pure state. Religious people believe that the presence of God or a supreme spirit can fill people, objects, and feelings with holiness. For example, a CHURCH, TEMPLE, or SYNAGOGUE is thought to be filled with holiness. Worshipers often treat such buildings with special religious respect and admiration.

HOLY MAN ✵ *See* GURU; PRIEST; SHAMAN.

HOME, RELIGION IN ✵ Almost all religions consider the home as a special place of PRAYER, celebration, and religious learning. The home is usually the place where children receive their first religious instruction, and absorb their religious attitudes. For example, in CONFUCIANISM the home is the place where the highest virtues of justice, politeness, honesty, and respect for parents are taught to the children. Some religions consider the home a special place of prayer. For example, in SHINTO, a shrine—a sacred space with a small ALTAR—is found in nearly every home. Some Christian homes reserve a short time every day, usually in the evening, for quiet FAMILY prayer and reflection. [*See also* CHRISTIANITY.]

HUMOR ✵ Fun and laughter that have a role in religion. Some serious religious traditions may look down upon humor in religion. Yet humor may have a positive role in religion. For example, people laughing to-

Holi

A wild, fun, and humorous FESTIVAL celebrated by Hindus once a year, under a spring full moon. One of the purposes of Holi is to recall the tricks that the childlike, mischievous god Krishna used to play on people when he was young. During this festival, Krishna is worshiped as a child, and even gets a swing to play on! Holi also makes good fun of the stories and MYTHS of Hindu religion. At this festival, people dance about with their clothes stained red, and laugh and sing, in honor of the wild, mischievous god Krishna. Holi reminds people that no matter how serious religion is, there is still some room for play and HUMOR.

gether help develop a sense of community. Humor has been a part of religious practices since ancient times. For example, in some Native American traditions, RITUAL CLOWNS followed serious priests and poked fun at the RITUALS. In the Middle Ages in Europe, a "boy bishop" was chosen on certain FESTIVALS. He was dressed in religious robes and made fun of the real CHURCH leaders. Today, Hindus honor the god Krishna by celebrating Holi, a festival that includes parades and wild fun. [*See also* HINDUISM; NATIVE AMERICAN RELIGIONS.]

HUNTING AND GATHERING SOCIETIES

Since the time that human beings first appeared on Earth, they have lived by hunting animals and gathering food from wild plants. About 35,000 years ago, modern humans first appeared. These early people painted pictures on the walls of caves, such as those in France and Spain. They also made small statues of women. Most scientists believe that these early hunters used the pictures and statues in hunting rituals to ask the GODS for success.

HYMN
A religious song of praise. Hymns are generally sung by the CONGREGATION or a CHOIR in Christian services. Hymns offer praise to God or to a saint. The words of the hymn are not taken from the BIBLE. While some hymns are more than 1,000 years old, others were written in recent years. The word *hymn* is sometimes used to refer to religious songs in general.

ICONS
See CLOTHING; IMAGES.

IMAGES
Paintings, drawings, or stained-glass pictures that show holy people or scenes. Some religions, such as CHRISTIANITY and BUDDHISM, often have many images in their places of worship. For example, members of EASTERN ORTHODOXY use special pictures of SAINTS called icons in their prayers. Other religions, such as ISLAM, teach that it is wrong to have images in a place of worship. They believe that people might worship the image instead of God.

An icon of Jesus with the Virgin Mary in Poland

INCARNATION
A process in which a GOD or a holy being comes to EARTH as a human or an animal. Incarnation is a central DOCTRINE in CHRISTIANITY. Christians believe that God was incarnated, or made man, in the person of Jesus. Incarnation is important to members of HINDUISM as well. Hindus believe that their god Vishnu was incarnated many times. Vishnu has come in the form of such creatures as a fish, a turtle, a dwarf, and one incarnation that is yet to come.

INDIA AND SOUTH ASIA
On the southern edge of Asia a huge triangle of land juts out into the Indian Ocean. This area is sometimes called the subcontinent of India. It holds five countries—India, Pakistan, Bangladesh, Nepal, and Sri Lanka.

Many of the world's religions started in South Asia. These include HINDUISM, BUDDHISM, JAINISM, and SIKHISM. People who practice other religions have also moved to South Asia, and they have brought their religions with them. Thus, ISLAM, CHRISTIANITY, ZOROASTRIANISM, and JUDAISM are also found on the subcontinent. Most of the world's Hindus live in India.

Problems have resulted from so many religions living side by side. In 1947 the former British colony of India was divided into two countries—a Muslim state called Pakistan and a secular state called India. (A secular state is a state in which the government has no religious affiliation.) Religious riots followed this partition, and many people died.

Since then India and Pakistan have fought wars and battles over whether the northern tip of South Asia, called Kashmir, should belong to India, to Pakistan, or be independent. Most of the people of Kashmir are Muslims, but the former king was a Hindu, and he gave Kashmir to India. On the island of Sri Lanka, Hindus called Tamils live in the north. Many of them have been fighting a war to be separate from the Buddhists who live in the south.

Styles of Worship. Many people in South Asia use statues or IMAGES in their worship. Hindus use statues of their GODS. Jains use statues of their SAINTS. Buddhists use statues of the Buddha.

In all three religions worshipers present OFFERINGS such as flowers to these statues. They may also burn lamps before them. But they have different ideas about what these acts mean. Hindus think that they are giving gifts directly to the gods. Buddhists often say they are remembering what the Buddha taught.

Hinduism and Buddhism also use techniques for meditating. Hindus often call meditation yoga.

A Hindu makes an offering at a shrine in South Asia.

Islam considers the use of images in worship to be a sin. Therefore, Muslims worship in ways that are quite different. They are supposed to pray five times a day facing MECCA. At noon on Friday they gather at a MOSQUE for special prayers and a SERMON. Christians in South Asia worship much like Christians in the United States.

Ethics. South Asian religions have given much attention to how people should act. The "five precepts" of Buddhism resemble the TEN COMMANDMENTS. They forbid killing, stealing, lying, and sexual misconduct. Jains teach that we should not hurt any living thing, not even tiny insects. They call this principle *ahimsa*. Hindus say that people born in different castes have different duties, which they call *dharma*.

Many religions in South Asia say that people should live a special kind of life in order to reach their highest religious goal. The few people who live such a life give up their property, homes, and families, wander from place to place, and beg for their food. Buddhists and Jains call such people MONKS AND NUNS. Hindus call them *sadhus* and *sadhvis*.

Architecture. South Asian architecture shows how people are religious. Hindus and Jains build TEMPLES. In northern India temples have tall, curving tops above their most sacred area. In southern India

Yoga

"Yoga" is a word that is related to the English word "yoke." It means much the same thing—to harness or restrain.

In Hinduism yoga has many different meanings. Sometimes it refers to any kind of religious practice. For example, a famous Hindu book, the BHAGAVAD GITA, says worshiping gods is a kind of yoga. It calls that yoga *bhakti*, or devotion.

People usually use the word *yoga* to mean something more specific. In NORTH AMERICA people often mean body and breathing exercises that are supposed to make a person more healthy. This yoga is called *hatha yoga*.

In another yoga, *rajayoga*, or royal yoga, people sit, concentrating their minds. They hope that they will experience a reality that does not change and will never end.

Some Hindus believe that the energy which makes all things live sleeps at the bottom of their spines. They use the exercises of "tantric yoga" to wake that energy up.

they have tall, richly decorated pyramids above the gates that lead into the sacred area.

Muslims do not build temples. They build mosques, which are

places to pray. In large cities, such as Lahore in Pakistan and Delhi in India the mosques are huge.

In Sri Lanka one often sees Buddhist *stupas*. These are large hemispherical mounds, topped with something like a giant golf tee. At them Buddhists recall the Buddha's teachings.

ISLAM ❧ A major world religion that began in MECCA, a city in what is now Saudi Arabia. The word *Islam* means submission to the will of God, or Allah. Muslims, or followers of Islam, believe that peace comes through submission to the will of God.

In the year 610 C.E. Muhammad (570–632 C.E.), who lived in Mecca, was visited by the angel Gabriel. Mohammad believed that the angel Gabriel brought messages from Allah. These messages called upon the people to submit to the will of Allah. Later, these messages were written down in the scared book of Islam, the QU'RAN, or Koran.

Teachings. Islam is a monotheistic religion. It teaches that there is only one God, Allah, who is the creator and ruler of HEAVEN AND EARTH. Muslims believe that Allah sent many great PROPHETS, including Abraham, Moses, and Jesus, to reveal God's will to human beings. The last and the greatest of God's prophets is Muhammad.

Muslims follow the *shariah*, the way or law of God. It is revealed in the Qu'ran and in the life and deeds of the Prophet Muhammad. The *shariah* affects all areas of life. These include art, education, diet, and politics. After death and on the day of judgment, Muslims believe that all people will be raised from the dead and be judged by Allah according to their actions on earth.

Practices. Duties known as the Five Pillars of Faith provide the foundation for the lives of Muslims. The first pillar, or duty, is to believe in God and Muhammad as his prophet. The second pillar is daily PRAYER. Muslims face Mecca and pray five times a day. At least once a week, Muslims gather in a MOSQUE, or house of worship, for a formal service with sermon. The third duty is giving aid to the poor. The fourth duty is fasting from dawn to sunset during *Ramadan*, a month in the lunar calendar used by Muslims.

The Great Mosque in Mecca, Saudi Arabia

Making a *hajj*, or pilgrimage, to Mecca is the fifth pillar of Islam. Muslims who are healthy and have enough money, are to travel to Mecca at least once in their lives. During the pilgrimage, Muslims visit the *Kaaba*, a large cube-shaped building that is the holiest of shrines for Muslims.

Forms of Islam. Islam is the major religion in most countries stretching from Morocco in North Africa to Indonesia in Southeast Asia. About 85 percent of Muslims follow the Sunni branch of Islam, and follow the customs of the prophet Muhammad. This group does not have special religious leaders. About 15 percent of Muslims, who mostly live in Iran, are Shiite Muslims. This group follows the leadership of Muhammad's descendents, called Imams.

Many Muslims are also followers of Sufis or mystical teachers. They stress that the oneness of God means that God is everywhere and can be felt by inner experience. Sufis are known for their poetry.

Islam has created a special culture. Its beauty can be seen in its great mosques. There are no pictures in them, for Muslims believe that God cannot be pictured. They also believe that pictures and statues distract from the worship of Allah. [*See also* ANGEL; END OF THE WORLD; MOON.]

The Life of Muhammad (570–632 C.E.)

The last PROPHET of Allah and a key figure in Islam. Muhammad was born in 570 C.E. in MECCA, a city in what is now Saudi Arabia. He was orphaned at an early age. At age 25, Muhammad married a businesswoman named Khadija. They had six children.

When Muhammad was in his thirties, he was visited by the ANGEL Gabriel. The angel brought Muhammad messages from God. Muhammad memorized Allah's words and eventually began to proclaim God's word to the people of Mecca. But the people of Mecca rejected Muhammad's teaching. Fearing for his life, Muhammad and his followers fled to the city of Medina. The escape to Medina is known as the *Hegira*. In 629 Muhammad returned to Mecca and his former enemies surrendered to him. Many people in Mecca became Muslims. Muhammad died in 632. After his death, Allah's messages to him were written down in the QU'RAN.

Muslims do not consider Muhammad the founder of Islam. He is Allah's final prophet. Other prophets include Abraham, Moses, and Jesus. Thus Muslims trace the origins of Islam to Abraham, rather than to Muhammad.

JAINISM ❧ A religion that started in India. It was founded about 2,500 years ago by a man named Mahavira. Mahavira believed that every human being has an eternal SOUL, or *jiva*, that is trapped in the world. The soul can be freed by living simply and in a way that does not harm life.

Those who follow Jainism are called Jains. (To pronounce "Jain" correctly, the "ai" should sound like the "ie" in the word "lie.") There are about 8 million Jains in the world today. They mostly live in India, but there are Jains in the United States and Great Britain, too. Many work in business—jobs that harm life as little as possible. Jain MONKS AND NUNS devote themselves to following a life of simplicity and non-harm.

Teachings. Jains believe that until a person's soul is freed, it will continue to be reborn in different bodies. In other words, people do not have just one life but a series of lives. This belief is called REINCARNATION. What happens to a person's soul when it is freed? According to Jainism, it floats to the very top of the universe. There it is filled with knowledge and happiness.

Jainism teaches that the universe has always existed. No God created it. Souls have always been trapped, but they can be freed by becoming less attached to the world. What this means, according to Jainism, is that people need to desire material things and comforts less. They need to live more simply. Then they will be happier and eventually their souls will become free.

Practices. Jains believe that when people desire material things and comforts they easily become aggressive and violent. This is why the the idea of nonviolence is so important to Jainism. Nonviolence is the way to become less attached to the world. Because Jains do not wish to harm animals, they are vegetarians. They eat neither meat nor fish.

Jain monks and nuns are especially careful not to harm life. They carry a brush to gently sweep insects out of their way when they walk or when they sit down. Some Jain monks believe that everything should be renounced, including clothing. They are called Digambara, which means "sky-clothed," or naked.

The Life of Mahavira (Fifth century B.C.E.)

Mahavira is the founder of JAINISM. He lived in the north of ancient India. It is thought that he lived at the same time as the Buddha, the founder of BUDDHISM.

Mahavira was born into a princely family. When Mahavira was 30 years old he wandered across northern India searching for the truth about life. He wore no clothes and ate very little. He was often silent, and would stand still like a statue. In this way Mahavira denied himself worldly pleasures. After 12 years, he freed his soul of attachment to the world. He knew that when he died his soul would not be reborn again.

Mahavira spent the rest of his life teaching and he started a community of MONKS AND NUNS. He is believed to have died at the age of 72.

This name is given to one of the two main traditions of Jainism. The other tradition is called Shvetambara, or "white-clothed," because their monks and nuns wear simple white robes. [*See also* BUDDHISM; HINDUISM; INDIA AND SOUTH ASIA; SIKHISM.]

JEHOVAH'S WITNESSES

A sect of CHRISTIANITY founded by Charles Russell in the late 1800s. The name describes the members of the group who witness, or explain their religious beliefs, about Jehovah, another name for God. Witnessing to people outside their religion is a large part of the work of Jehovah's Witnesses. They often go door to door to witness. They believe in living moral, virtuous lives in order to prepare themselves for God's judgment. In general, the group does not interact with other religious denominations. They also try to stay completely separate from the government. For example, they do not salute the flag, join the military, or vote in elections.

JUDAISM

The oldest religion to practice monotheism, the worship of one God. Jews trace their roots back almost 4,000 years, to a special pact, or *covenant*, between God and Abraham. Jews believe they are Abraham's descendants.

History. Jews were once slaves in Egypt, and were then known as *Israelites*. The BIBLE says that Moses freed the Israelites and led them to a promised land. They called this land Judah (modern Israel) and they called themselves Jews. The Jews worshiped God with PRAYER and SACRIFICE in a Temple in Jerusalem. The Babylonians, enemies of the Jews,

Jews go to Jerusalem's Western Wall to pray.

destroyed this Temple in 586 B.C.E. The Jews rebuilt their Temple, but then the Romans destroyed it again in 70 C.E. Jews were scattered from their promised land to many different places, and since then Jews have lived all over the world. Sometimes Jews suffered PERSECUTION because they were different from the people around them. The worst time was during World War II, when about 6 million Jews were killed by the Nazis in the *Holocaust.*

Practices and Beliefs. Since the destruction of the second Temple, most Jews practice their religion in local CONGREGATIONS under the leadership of RABBIS. Some PRAYERS and ceremonies, like the reading of the TORAH, are celebrated in the SYNAGOGUE. Other ceremonies take place at home. Major Jewish festivals commemorate God's relationship with Jews and the world. These include the weekly day of rest (or *Sabbath,* on Saturday), the New Year (Rosh Hashanah), the Day of Atonement (Yom Kippur), and Passover (Pesah)—celebrating freedom from slavery.

Some Jews strictly observe RITUAL commandments, or *halakah.* They follow special FOOD laws, known as *kashrut,* and cannot eat certain foods, such as pork. The food they eat is approved by rabbis. They do not work or drive on the Sabbath and they pray in Hebrew.

Other Jews emphasize prayer and spiritual life. For them it is most important to do good deeds. They believe Jews should work to heal the world's social problems. Many Jews believe that at the END OF THE WORLD God will send a special messenger, a MESSIAH, who will rebuild the Temple in Jerusalem and make the world perfect.

There are many different types of Jews: Reform, Conservative, and Orthodox Jews are the most common in North America. These groups disagree about *halakah* and religious observance. Another large group of

The Life of Moses (Fourteenth century B.C.E)

Moses was born around 3,000 years ago when the Israelites were enslaved in Egypt. When he was a baby, his parents gave him away to keep him safe, and he was raised by the Pharaoh of Egypt. God appeared to Moses and told him to lead the Jews out of slavery. Moses performed many MIRACLES in God's name, including bringing ten plagues, or disasters, to Egypt. Through Moses, God spoke to the Jews and gave them the TEN COMMANDMENTS and other rules for religious life. Moses led the Jews to their promised land but died before the people entered it. Jews revere Moses because he spoke directly with God, freed them from slavery, and gave them special laws and rules.

Jews is the *Hasidim*, who practice a form of Jewish MYSTICISM, dress differently, and live apart from non-Jews. There are around 14 million Jews in the world today, mostly in the United States and Israel.

JUDGMENT, FINAL ⚜ *See* END OF THE WORLD.

KARMA ⚜ According to the beliefs of HINDUISM and BUDDHISM, a person's actions, taken together, in any one life. Hindus and Buddhists believe that an endless string of lives, and their karma, or good and evil actions, in one life causes things that happen to them in the next life. For example, injury at work or a chance meeting with a stranger who becomes a friend, are the products of the karma of a person's previous life. People's looks, their intelligence, what they own, how long they live, and whether they have been reborn as a human being rather than an animal or a plant, is caused by the karma of their previous life. [*See also* AFTERLIFE; REINCARNATION.]

KINGSHIP ⚜ A position of leadership in some cultures. Some tribes or groups of people believed that their leader had special holy powers. For example, some tribes in Africa believed in a rainmaker-king who controlled the weather and the harvest. In other cultures, people believed that their king was a god. For example, the pharaohs of ancient Egypt were thought to be divine. Still other cultures believed that their leader spoke for a divine being. For example, Mongolians believed that their king was sent from heaven to carry out God's will. The role of sacred kingship usually involved protecting people from natural disasters, diseases, and enemies. In some cases, the king was also the religious leader of the community.

LANGUAGES, RELIGIOUS ℵ

A special language used in services, ceremonies, or SCRIPTURES. For example, in ROMAN CATHOLICISM some services are held in Latin. Latin is the language of the Romans who were among the first to practice Christianity. Hebrew is the religious language for JUDAISM. Jews use Hebrew for special prayers and religious ceremonies. It is the language of the Jewish scriptures. Sanskrit is the religious language in HINDUISM. It is the language of very old religious texts.

LATTER-DAY SAINTS ℵ

Members of a DENOMINATION of CHRISTIANITY, often called Mormons. The Church of Latter-Day Saints was founded by a PROPHET named Joseph Smith (1805–1844). Today, the largest group of Latter-Day Saints lives in Utah. Latter-Day Saints have their own translation of the BIBLE. They also follow another sacred text, *The Book of Mormon*, by Joseph Smith. They believe that the three persons of the TRINITY are three different Gods, not one God as most Christians believe. They also believe that God speaks to them through the president of their church. Latter-Day Saints usually do not smoke or drink alcohol, coffee, or tea. They value hard work and they require most young men and women to spend 18 months as MISSIONARIES doing good works outside their religious community.

LAW, RELIGIOUS ℵ

Rules set up by religious TRADITION or authority. In traditional societies, the basic laws of the land were believed to have come from a divine source. Today, religious law is taught and upheld by religious groups like Christian CHURCHES, the Hindu priesthood, or Jewish SYNAGOGUES. It is followed by people who accept it voluntarily. Thus, whether or not one works on Sunday, the Sabbath, or a holy day in accordance with a religious law depends on one's personal belief. However, some religious FUNDAMENTALISTS believe that the government should enforce some religious laws, especially on matters of ETHICS.

LIBERALISM, RELIGIOUS ℵ

Religion interpreted in a free and open way. Liberal thought in many religions has stressed looking at scripture and religious practice so that it fits with the best current science and philosophy. Religious liberals also often want to use religion as a guide for social change. They often try to make it more democratic and allow more individual choice.

LIGHT ℵ

An important SYMBOL in religion. In nearly all religions, light is thought of as coming from God or the GODS, or as a sign of GOOD. In ZOROASTRIANISM, for example, light has been created by the good SPIRIT, while darkness has been created by the EVIL spirit. In JUDAISM, CHRISTIANITY, and ISLAM, light is the first creation of God, as recorded in the first book of the BIBLE. Candles, oil lamps, or torches are used in nearly all religions to show the presence of the holy. In the Hindu marriage ceremony, the young couple at marriage must walk around a sacred FIRE, which stands for life, as a sign of their desire to have children.

A young girl lights the eighth candle on the menorah.

Hanukkah

In JUDAISM, the eight-day celebration each December of the rededication of the TEMPLE. Also known as the Festival of Lights. In 165 B.C.E. enemies of the Jews captured the Temple and dishonored it by making it into a pagan temple. Three years later the Jews recaptured it and wished to rededicate it—purify it of its dishonor. However, only one small vessel of the sacred oil was found. Hanukkah (Hebrew for "dedication") recalls the miracle of the small amount of oil that burned for eight whole days, the time necessary for the rededication. Hanukkah today is celebrated by the lighting of the menorah, the eight-branched candlestick kept in the Jewish home. A new candle is lit each night of Hanukkah until all eight candles are burning.

MAKKA ❧ *See* MECCA.

MECCA ❧ A city in Saudi Arabia, the birthplace of the prophet Muhammad. Mecca is the holiest of the cities of ISLAM. Muhammad received his original revelation of the QU'RAN from the ANGEL Gabriel in a cave outside Mecca. Muslims everywhere in the world face Mecca when saying their daily prayers. Muhammad's escape from his enemies, from Mecca to the city of Medina, is known as the Hijrah. Each year, more than a million Muslims make a PILGRIMAGE to Mecca during the last month of the Islamic calendar. [*See also* PROPHETS.]

MEDIUMSHIP ❧ The attempt to mediate or go between ordinary people and the spiritual world and connect them in some way. Mediums often call upon the souls of the dead to reveal hidden knowledge, and they often claim to foretell the future. Some people believe that the souls of the dead communicate with the living through mediums. A medium usually speaks or acts while in a TRANCE. Mediumship is very much like a modern form of shamanism. [*See also* SHAMANS; SUPERNATURAL.]

MESSIAH ❧ The person for whom a religious group waits. The Messiah will free the faithful from suffering. In JUDAISM, the Messiah is a king who will be sent by God. Members of CHRISTIANITY believe that Jesus Christ was the king, or Messiah, whom the Jews await. Members of ISLAM believe that the *Mahdi* will come at the end of time and bring faith in God and order to the world. Buddhists believe that the Buddha

A nativity scene showing the birth of Jesus

Christmas

The Christian holy day that celebrates the birth of Jesus, the Christian's MESSIAH. For most of CHRISTIANITY, Christmas is celebrated on December 25. Some EASTERN ORTHODOX traditions celebrate Christmas later in December or in early January. Christians remember that Mary and Joseph, Jesus' parents, rode to the town of Bethlehem and could find only a manger, or animal barn, for shelter. When Jesus was born, three wise men followed a bright star to the manger. They brought royal gifts to Jesus.

Today Christmas is a time of great celebration. Families exchange gifts, sing Christmas carols, eat festive meals, and some attend a midnight CHURCH service.

will be reborn as *Maitreya* and will lead Buddhists to freedom.

METHODISTS ❧ A DENOMINATION of PROTESTANTISM founded in England by John Wesley (1703–91) in the late 1700s. Methodists believe that the most important part of religion is having a personal relationship with God. Methodist services include a SERMON, PRAYERS, sometimes Communion, and HYMNS. Today there are several branches of the Methodist church. The largest denomination is the United Methodist Church. Certain other major denominations are predominantly African American, including the African Methodist Episcopal Church and the African Methodist Episcopal Zion Church.

MEXICO AND CENTRAL AMERICA ❧ Mexico and Central America stretch south from the United States to Panama. The religious culture in this part of the world comes from two main sources. These are the native peoples' religious beliefs and practices and the ROMAN CATHOLICISM that the Spaniards brought in the early 1500s.

Unlike what happened in the British colonies farther north, the Spaniards did not push native peoples ("Indians") off the land. Instead, they forced native people to work the land for them. This practice had at least two important results. First, many Christians in Mexico and Central America have ancestors who were native people. Their practice of CHRISTIANITY has many elements that come from the religions of their ancestors.

Second, people whose heritage is Spanish or mixed Spanish and Indian tend to be rich. People of native ancestry tend to be poor. The divide between rich and poor is sometimes very large.

A Catholic church in Veracruz, Mexico

Heroes and Saints. Like Catholics in other countries, Catholics in Mexico and Central America give honor to SAINTS. Mexicans especially give honor to Our Lady of Guadalupe. Guadalupe is a northeastern suburb of Mexico City.

In 1531 Juan Diego, a poor Aztec farmer, claimed that Mary, the mother of Jesus, had appeared to him. He told the bishop that she wanted a church built in the place where she had appeared, now Guadalupe. At first the bishop did not believe him. Several days later, Juan returned to the bishop's palace with roses that he said Mary told him to put in his cape. When he opened the cape, he found on it a miraculous image of Mary in the form of a native Mexican. The bishop was now convinced that Mary really was appearing to Juan Diego and had a church built in Guadalupe. The cape can still be seen there today.

Our Lady of Guadalupe is a Catholic saint, but in form she is similar to the Goddess Tonantzin, whom the Aztecs worshiped before the Spaniards came. During the war of independence, she became a symbol of free Mexico. Today more Mexicans make a PILGRIMAGE to Guadalupe than to any other holy site.

Ethics. The Catholic church teaches people in Mexico and Central America how they are supposed to live. In addition, the traditional stories of Maya and other native peoples teach how to live. For example, the twin boy heroes of the Maya epic, *Popol Vuh*, illustrate the virtue of cleverness. They need to outwit various evil beings, including death.

Poverty presents major ethical problems in Mexico and Central America. Over the centuries close connections between the Catholic church and the wealthy have resulted in much "anti-clericalism," or opposition to the officials of the church. In the 1960s, 1970s, and 1980s, a group of priests wanted to help the poor. They developed a way of thinking that they called "liberation theology."

Liberation theology disturbed many people, including the wealthy and powerful in Central America, leaders of the Catholic church in Rome, and the United States government. In some cases people working for the poor used violence. In many more cases people in power

Quinceañera, a Celebration for Girls

The *Quinceañera* is a RITE OF PASSAGE for girls. The celebration goes back to the time before the Spaniards arrived in Mexico and Central America. Today it is celebrated in the SOUTHWESTERN UNITED STATES, too.

The name Quinceañera comes from *quince años*, Spanish for "fifteen years." The Quinceañera marks a girl's fifteenth birthday, when she becomes a young woman.

For a time before her fifteenth birthday a girl is supposed to go to church and receive instructions on the roles and responsibilities of a woman. On the day of her birthday she dresses in a special dress, similar to a wedding dress. Relatives gather together, and they go to church for a special Mass. After the Mass the parents give a party in the young girl's honor. It generally includes music and dancing.

In earlier times the Quinceañera made a girl eligible for marriage. Today, girls do not usually marry so young, but some people believe a Quinceañera makes a girl eligible to date. In the United States Quinceañera celebrations have become very expensive.

used violence against those working for the poor.

One of the most important people killed in this struggle was the archbishop of El Salvador, Oscar Romero. He was assassinated while saying Mass in 1980.

Architecture. Mexico and Central America have very many impressive religious monuments. Some date from before the arrival of the Spaniards. Examples include the ancient pyramids at Teotihuacan and Chichen Itza and the Great Temple of the Aztecs, whose ruins construction workers discovered in Mexico City.

Mexico and Central America also have large Christian monuments. Examples include the Metropolitan Cathedral in Mexico City and the Basilica of Our Lady of Guadalupe.

MIDDLE EAST ✺ The Middle East is the area where three continents come together—EUROPE, Asia, and AFRICA. Today it is the home of such countries as Egypt, Israel, Iraq, and Saudi Arabia.

The Middle East has a long history. It is where people first started growing plants for food about 12,000 years ago. It is also where people built the first cities, and where they invented writing and money. The Middle East is also where three important religions began—JUDAISM, CHRISTIANITY, and ISLAM.

The Holy City of Jerusalem and Three Faiths

Three Faiths—JUDAISM, CHRISTIANITY, and ISLAM—all consider Jerusalem to be a holy city.

For Jews, Jerusalem is the center of the land of Israel. It was also the location of God's Temple, which the Romans destroyed in 70 C.E. Today, remains of that Temple can be seen in the western wall of the Temple Mount. This is an especially important place for Jews to pray.

For Christians, Jerusalem is important because there Jesus suffered, died, was buried and, as Christians believe, rose again and appeared to his followers. According to tradition, a Church of the Holy Sepulcher stands at the place where Jesus was buried.

For Muslims, Jerusalem is the third most sacred city in the world. (Mecca and Medina are more sacred, because they are more directly associated with God's final revelation through the prophet Muhammad.) According to one story, God transported Muhammad to Jerusalem one night on a winged horse named Buraq. From there Muhammad ascended into heaven. (He came down the same night.) An ancient mosque, the Dome of the Rock, marks the spot where his ascent began.

These three religions are alike in many ways. They share the same stories about Adam and Eve, Noah and the FLOOD, Abraham, Sarah and Hagar, and their sons Isaac and Ishmael. They also look at the world the same way. They believe that there is one God—usually a "He" rather than a "She"—who created the world. This God teaches people how to live. He speaks to them through people called PROPHETS, and His words are contained in a holy book. At the end of time He will judge people based on their actions on earth. Some will go to HEAVEN, but some will go to HELL. Another thing that all three religions have in common is the holy city of Jerusalem.

The most widespread religion in the Middle East today is Islam. But Israel is a Jewish state and Christians also live in Middle Eastern countries.

(continues on page 73)

A Christian church (left) and the Dome of the Rock (right, background) in the old city of Jerusalem

MIDWESTERN UNITED STATES

✤ The Midwest is the heartland of the United States. It stretches from the Appalachian Mountains in the east to the Great Plains in the west.

People of European ancestry settled the Midwestern United States during the 1800s. In the early 1800s they generally settled on the land as individuals or isolated families. Later immigrants tended to settle in larger groups.

At first the earliest settlers showed little interest in religion. They had left the churches of the east coast behind, and no institution on the frontier took their place. That changed with the coming of the camp meeting revival, an emotional religious gathering held by METHODISTS and BAPTISTS. These revivals influenced many people to become Methodists and Baptists.

Unlike the earliest settlers, many later settlers in the Midwest did not have to find a new religion on the frontier. They continued to practice their old religions. For example, many Dutch immigrants settled in western Michigan. They made that region a stronghold of the Dutch REFORMED CHURCH. Many Scandinavians settled in Minnesota and the Dakotas. They brought their Lutheran heritage with them. Today Lutherans make up more than one-third of the population of Minnesota and the Dakotas. Large numbers of Lutherans live in Wisconsin, Montana, Nebraska, and Iowa, as well as in Illinois and Pennsylvania.

The coming of European settlers disrupted the lives of the Native Americans already living in the Midwest. Eventually the United States government confined the native peoples of the Great Plains to reservations, such as Pine Ridge reservation in South Dakota. Many Native Americans converted to Christianity. Some of them also preserve older religious traditions.

Besides European Protestants and Native Americans, many Catholics live in the Midwest. Jews are fewer in number. Cincinnati is, however, an important center for Reform Judaism.

Especially in the late 1900s, immigrants from Asia and the MIDDLE EAST brought HINDUISM, BUDDHISM, ISLAM, and other religions to the Midwestern United States. Most of them live in large cities, like Chicago and St. Louis.

Styles of Worship. In the southern Midwest worship practices often resemble those of the SOUTHERN UNITED STATES. They emphasize the rousing preaching associated with EVANGELICALISM, or "born again" Christianity.

Worship in the Lutheran tradition in the upper Midwest is more restrained. Throughout the 1800s Lutherans tended to worship in the languages of their homelands—Ger-

Celebrating St. Lucia's Day is a Lutheran tradition in parts of the Midwest.

man, Swedish, Norwegian, Danish, or others—rather than in English. That meant that Lutherans from one country could not worship together with Lutherans from another.

Lutheran worship is much like Catholic worship. Lutherans have, however, a centuries-old tradition of congregations singing HYMNS. (Roman Catholicism began to emphasize singing hymns only after the second VATICAN COUNCIL in the 1960s.) As a result, many of the hymns Lutherans sing are centuries old, such as Martin Luther's hymn, "A Mighty Fortress Is Our God."

The Native Americans of the Plains also traditionally practice what is called the VISION quest. It is not as common now as it was in the 1800s. As boys start to mature, they go off by themselves. They do not eat. Instead, they meditate. They hope to receive a vision that will guide them throughout life. One of the most elaborate visions ever received appears in the book, *Black Elk Speaks*.

Ethics and Family Life. Midwesterners divide on many ethical issues. Some insist on traditional ways of living. Others are more tolerant of change. A good example is the role of women in churches. Women have traditionally done many jobs in churches. But before the twentieth century most churches did not allow women to be priests or ordained ministers.

Architecture. The Midwestern United States has many CHURCHES and SYNAGOGUES built in traditional styles. For example, old churches on the Great Plains were simple wooden buildings, usually with a steeple at the entrance. Some of them are still in existence. Rockefeller Chapel at the University of Chicago is a Gothic church. The Cathedral-Basilica of Saint Louis is built in a style called Byzantine. It contains more mosaics than any other church in the world.

Other Midwestern churches and synagogues are more distinctive. They are built in the modern styles of the twentieth century. From a distance, the Prayer Tower at Oral Roberts University in Tulsa, Oklahoma, looks like a giant cross. But the cross-bar is really a circle. The Midwest also contains many modern synagogues. The first such synagogue built in the United States, the synagogue of B'nai Amoona congregation in St. Louis, was designed by Eric Mendelsohn and dedicated in 1950. It now houses the St. Louis Center of Contemporary Arts.

Between World War I and World War II Midwestern Muslim communities built MOSQUES in Ross, South Dakota, and Cedar Rapids, Iowa. Many Midwestern cities, including Toledo, Ohio, and Detroit, Michigan, have impressive mosques. In the last part of the twentieth century Buddhists, Hindus, and other religious groups also began to build religious structures in Midwestern cities. One example is the Zoroastrian center in suburban Chicago. [*See also* ZOROASTRIANISM.]

Religion on the Frontier

In the late 1700s, people living on the east coast of the United States began to cross the Appalachian mountains. Life on the frontier was different from what they had known on the east coast. Fewer people lived there, and they lived much farther apart. There were no religious institutions, such as churches. Communities were not really big enough to start or support churches, either.

As the frontier became more settled, some Christian groups felt called upon to bring their faith to the people. These were evangelical or born-again Christians. Two groups of evangelicals worked on the frontier—Baptists and Methodists. Both groups stressed believing in the BIBLE.

Evangelical preachers on the frontier created a new kind of cultural event. It was called the *camp meeting revival*. People traveled to a place, sometimes 30 or 40 miles (48 or 64 kilometers) away, and camped. They sang, prayed, and listened to preachers who stirred up their emotions.

The camp meeting was also a social event—a chance to see other people, learn the latest news, and buy much-needed supplies.

(continued from page 69)

Religious Literature. For Jews and Christians the most important book is the BIBLE. For this reason Muslims call them "People of the Book."

For Muslims the most important book is the QU'RAN. It contains the words of God, given in perfect form to the prophet MUHAMMAD.

The Qu'ran is very important in the Middle East. Muslims refer to the Qu'ran often, and some memorize every word of it. Teachers of the Qu'ran are important leaders in the community.

Heroes and Saints. The most important religious heroes in the Middle East have been prophets. These are people through whom God speaks. For Muslims the most important prophet was Muhammad. Christians believe that the most important person, Jesus, was more than a prophet. He was the Son of God.

Scholars who interpret the Qu'ran or the Bible also have important roles as leaders in the Middle East. Jurists or legal scholars study the Qu'ran and other traditions and teach Muslims the proper way to live. Rabbis study the Bible and Talmud and do the same for Jews.

Prayer. In the Middle East as in other parts of the world, PRAYER is an important way that Jews, Christians, and Muslims worship God.

Muslims pray five times a day. As God instructs in the Qu'ran, they face the city of MECCA in Saudi Arabia. In praying, Muslims stand, sit, and bow down to God.

In the Middle East one often hears a voice in the distance announcing that it is time to pray. The chant or music of the "call to prayer" marks the different parts of the day.

Art and Architecture. Islam teaches that no one should make pictures or statues of people or animals. As a result, art and architecture in the Middle East have a distinctive look. Muslim artists make pictures and decorate buildings with complicated geometrical shapes and plant designs. They also take sayings from the Qu'ran and the names of God revealed in the Qu'ran and decorate them as a way of showing their devotion.

MINISTER ❧ The title of a leading church official or pastor in PROTESTANTISM. A minister performs many church functions, including church services, marriages, funerals, church administration, and preaching, teaching, and counseling. Usually ministers have received a special education for the job. They are also ordained in a special ceremony.

MIRACLES ❧ Events that seem to be impossible. Miracles are thought to be the acts of God in order to inspire FAITH. A miracle might be seen in a part of a natural event. For example, when the lava from a volcano in Bali did not destroy a Hindu TEMPLE in its path, some people believed this was a miracle. Special people chosen by God may also perform miracles. For example, many SAINTS have saved the dying. Jesus and saints of many religions performed miracles such as healing the sick, casting out demons, and other remarkable feats.

MISSIONARIES
Religious people who try to bring others to their religion. Some religions, such as Methodism and the LATTER-DAY SAINTS, have many missionaries. Others, such as JUDAISM, do not have any. Missionaries believe that it is important to bring others to their religion through CONVERSION. They often go to foreign countries to spread their message. Many missionaries build hospitals and schools and work to help the poor, the sick, and the needy.

MONKS AND NUNS
Religious men and women who take religious vows and live in communities. Usually they do not marry or have families. Centuries ago, most Christian monks and nuns prayed for the rest of the members of their FAITH. Today, most monks and nuns are active in society. For example, some monks and nuns in CHRISTIANITY run

Missionary nuns follow the rules of religious order.

schools, hospitals, or services for the poor. Monks and nuns usually follow special religious rules. These rules may include daily prayer, fasting, and certain rituals. Some religions, such as JUDAISM, do not have communities of monks or nuns. [*See also* RELIGIOUS ORDERS.]

MONOTHEISM
See POLYTHEISM.

MOON
An important symbol in religion for ages. It has particularly been associated with WOMEN, the sea, and WATER in general. It has been considered the divine giver of rain. In many cultures the full moon was a time for meetings and FESTIVALS, and often a symbol of unending life. The Buddha, the founder of BUDDHISM, was said to have reached en-

The moon has long been a religious symbol.

lightenment, or a higher state of being, on a night of the full moon. The moon is also used in religious CALENDARS. For example, the Islamic calendar is lunar, and the Jewish Passover and Christian Easter are dated from the first full moon after the vernal equinox, or about March 21. [*See also* CHRISTIANITY; ISLAM; JUDAISM.]

MORMONS ⚜ *See* LATTER-DAY SAINTS.

MOUNTAINS ⚜ Important religious SYMBOLS in many cultures. Some people believe that mountains are GODS or ANCESTORS. For example, the Native Americans of the Pacific Northwest believe that Mount Rainier is a powerful ancestor. Some mountains are holy places where gods reveal themselves or where people may have VISIONS. Jews believe that God gave Moses the TEN COMMANDMENTS on Mount Sinai.

Muslims believe that the Prophet Muhammad received their holy book, the QU'RAN, on Mount Hira. Therefore these two mountains are very sacred places for Jews and Muslims. [*See also* BUDDHISM; HINDUISM; ISLAM; JAINISM; JUDAISM; NATIVE AMERICAN RELIGIONS.]

MUSLIM ⚜ *See* ISLAM.

MYSTERY RELIGIONS ⚜ Secret religious cults in ancient Mediterranean religions. People who practiced mystery religions promised not to speak to others about the RITUALS of their cult. Mystery religions often had private ceremonies when members were sworn to secrecy. An old Greek mystery religion worshipped the GODDESS Demeter and her daughter Persephone.

MYSTICISM ⚜ The search for deep spiritual truth. People who practice mysticism try to become one with the divine or with sacred ideas. Mystics attempt to bring about special intense and personal religious feelings. They practice opening their spirit and mind to mystical experience.

MYTHS ⚜ Very old stories about the beginning of the world and the human race. Myths offer societies an explanation of the world around them, and especially of why there is so much GOOD and EVIL in the world.

N O

NATIVE AMERICAN RELIGIONS

The religions practiced by the native peoples of North and South AMERICA. Native Americans have a deep religious connection with NATURE. Many call the EARTH *Mother Earth*. Many Native American ceremonies are dedicated to maintaining a harmonious balance with nature. Some Native American groups believe that animals have SPIRITS. When they hunt these animals, they perform ceremonies out of respect for the animals' spirit. For example, the North American Plateau Indians celebrate the arrivval of the salmon with special RITUALS. They throw the fish bones back into the water to make sure the salmon come back the next year. The Inca of South America believed in *huaca*, or spirits in the form of local stones and mountains. Religious leaders called SHAMANS, or medicine women and men, have special connections with the spirits. [*See also* NORTH AMERICA; SWEAT LODGES; VISIONS.]

Eagle dancers on the Alaskan coast

NATURE

An important source of religious SYMBOLS for cultures all over the world. Nature is everything that is not made by humans. Trees, rocks, plants, animals, the ocean, the SUN and the MOON are all a part of nature. Throughout history, people have attached religious meaning to nature. Some people believed that trees, rocks, and MOUNTAINS are GODS. For example, the Inca of South America believed that rocks and mountains are actually SPIRITS. Other groups believed that the sun and the moon were gods. Even today, certain holy days, including Ramadan, Passover, and Easter, are determined by the lunar calendar. [*See also* NATIVE AMERICAN RELIGIONS.]

NEW AGE RELIGIONS ✧
Modern groups calling for a complete change in people's awareness of the spiritual part of their lives. New Age religions are very different from traditional religions. They see the coming *new age* as a world of much greater happiness and concern for others. New Age religions use self-healing, natural foods, special music, crystals, acupuncture, and the occult to teach spiritual awareness. New Age religions usually believe in life beyond our planet and REINCARNATION. [*See also* MUSIC; OCCULTISM.]

NEW RELIGIOUS MOVEMENTS ✧
Religions that have arisen recently. Thousands of new religious movements have started in the twentieth century. Some began within older religions and some are entirely original. Typically they begin with the teaching of a PROPHET or FOUNDER who claims to have a new teaching from God. Usually a spiritual practice, like a method of HEALING or MEDITATION, is part of the message. Often the new religious movement appears during a time of confusion and rapid change. The movement tries to help people live with the new situation religiously. New religious movements sometimes attempt to bring TRADITION up to date, in harmony with current ways of life. One example is PENTECOSTALISM, which presents traditional Christianity with a new emphasis on spiritual healing and religious EXPERIENCE. It has free and open forms of organization that have led to its rapid growth around the world. A form of BUDDHISM in Japan, Soka Gakkai, emphasizes just one practice—a chant that is said to bring benefits to its modern-minded followers.

NEW TESTAMENT ✧
The second part of the Christian BIBLE. The New Testament was written up to one hundred years after the death of Jesus. The New Testament is made up of several types of works. The books of Matthew, Mark, Luke, and John are called the Gospels. They tell of Jesus' life, teachings, and death. The book of Acts tells the history of the CHURCH after Jesus. Many letters from DISCIPLES, called epistles, tell about spreading the message of Jesus. Finally, the book of Revelation foretells what will happen at the end of time.

NEW YEAR'S CELEBRATION ✧
A ceremony or FESTIVAL held to celebrate the beginning of the year. In many cultures, such as that of the ancient Babylonians, the New Year has been celebrated at the time of the spring planting. In JUDAISM, the New Year comes in September or October, after the harvest, with the celebration of Rosh Hashanah. The

A lion mask used in a Chinese New Year's festival

Chinese New Year, with its parades, theater, and other expressions of joy, is celebrated in January or February. In the Middle Ages, the Christian New Year was observed on March 25, the feast day of the Angel's announcement to Mary that she would bear the Son of God. Today in the Western world, New Year's celebrations are usually non-religious. [*See also* HOLIDAYS.]

NORTH AMERICA ✻ North America stretches from Panama to the far north of CANADA, but this entry concentrates on religion in the United States and Canada. Almost every religion in the world can be found in these two countries.

The oldest North Americans are the Native Americans, sometimes called Indians. Their ancestors came to North America about 40,000 years ago.

Native Americans have belonged to many different groups, such as Pueblo, Lakota, Kwakiutl, Iroquois, and Inuit. Each group has had its own way of life and religion.

Today, Native Americans in the United States and Canada are struggling with two key questions. The first centers on *traditionalism*, or how best to preserve their traditions. The second question deals with *assimilation* or how much to live like non-native neighbors. The assimilationists are likely to practice a form of Christianity, but traditionalists try to preserve ancient religious practices and to revive those that have been lost. For example, in the early 1970s an old leader, Henry Crow Dog, taught traditional RITUALS to young members of the American Indian Movement who were seeking their religious roots. Many traditionalists also want to get their sacred lands back, such as the Black Hills in South Dakota.

In the 1600s Europeans started settling lands that became the United States and Canada. Thus, most North Americans practice the religions brought by these European settlers, most often a kind of CHRISTIANITY. Few European settlers practiced JUDAISM, but today more Jews live in North America than anywhere else in the world, except Israel. The first Jews settled in North America in 1654.

Settlers from different parts of EUROPE brought with them different kinds of Christianity. Episcopalians, Puritans, Baptists, and QUAKERS came from England; Presbyterians came from Scotland; Lutherans came from Germany, among other places, along with the Mennonites, the AMISH, and the Brethren.

Canada was originally settled by the French. The Catholic church remains strong there, especially in Quebec. Starting in the 1800s, large numbers of Catholics came to the United States from Ireland, Italy, France, and other countries. As a result, the Roman Catholic church has been the largest single Christian group in the United States for about 150 years.

Not all forms of Christianity in North America came from Europe. Some developed in America, in part as a result of revivals. LATTER-DAY SAINTS, Seventh Day Adventists, and Holiness Churches arose in the mid-1800s. PENTECOSTALISM and FUNDA-MENTALISM arose in the early 1900s.

Africans who came to North America in the days of slavery generally lost their traditional religions. They became Christians, as the slave-holders wanted. They did not, however, simply imitate European Christianity. They created their own forms of worship. For example, the kind of religious song known as the

(continues on page 84)

Iroquois Federation

The Iroquois Federation joined together six Native American nations living in New York state: Mohawk, Oneida, Onondaga, Cayuga, Seneca, and Tuscarora. The traditional religion of the federation has several parts.

One aspect is the Longhouse Religion. It gets its name from the buildings in which Iroquois lived and performed rituals. Longhouse rituals take place every year, especially in midwinter. In this ritual, the Iroquois give thanks for blessings enjoyed in the past and get ready for the next year.

Another part of Iroquois religion is the medicine society. These groups of people have special RITUALS for healing diseases. There are women's societies as well as men's.

Dreams and VISIONS are also important in Iroquois religion. They give information and messages from the spirit world. The most important Iroquois to receive such messages was Handsome Lake (1735–1815), a prophet of the Seneca. Many Iroquois still practice the traditional religion.

NORTHEASTERN UNITED STATES ⚘

The heart of the northeastern United States is New England—Massachusetts, Connecticut, Rhode Island, Vermont, New Hampshire, and Maine. To the south and west of New England is the Mid-Atlantic region—New York, New Jersey, Delaware, and Pennsylvania. Maryland is between the Mid-Atlantic region and the SOUTHERN UNITED STATES.

The Puritans first settled New England in the 1620s. Their religious ideas have influenced the views of many Americans, including Americans' views about the United States.

In the 1700s and 1800s some descendants of the Puritans became Congregationalists. Others became Unitarians. Unitarians get their name because they believe Jesus was just a man, not God, and that God is a unity (one), not a TRINITY. They tend to be liberal, and most of them live in New England.

Starting in the 1800s many people came to the northeastern United States from Italy, Ireland, Poland, and other Catholic countries. As a result, ROMAN CATHOLICISM is now strong there. More than half of the people who live in Massachusetts are Catholic. So are more than one-third of the people who live in New Hampshire, Vermont, New York, and New Jersey.

Immigrants have brought other religions to the northeastern United States, too, especially in the 1900s. As a result, the northeastern United States is one of the world's most important centers of JUDAISM. New York City contains people who practice religions from all over the world.

Some religions started in the northeastern United States as well.

A typical New England church in New Hampshire

For example, Joseph Smith, the prophet of the LATTER-DAY SAINTS, or Mormons, translated the Book of Mormon in upstate New York. Mary Baker Eddy started CHRISTIAN SCIENCE in Boston. The Theosophical Society began in New York City in 1875.

Styles of Worship. Puritan worship was very simple. Puritans did not allow musical instruments in church. They sang psalms in unison, prayed, and listened to a SERMON. The worship of the QUAKERS, who have traditional roots in Pennsylvania, is simpler still.

In a Quaker meeting, people sit in silence. They wait for the Holy Spirit to speak in someone's heart.

The Catholic Mass is very different. It centers around a ritual meal called the Eucharist, or Holy Communion. The worship services of ANGLICAN and ORTHODOX Christians center around the Eucharist, too. In some Catholic Masses, as well as in services of "high church" Anglicans and Orthodox Christians, the PRIEST or priests wear richly decorated robes. Processions, MUSIC sung by

Puritans in New England

Puritans were the first English settlers in New England. Puritans called Pilgrims founded Plymouth, Massachusetts, in 1620. Other Puritans founded Boston in 1630. Still others settled Connecticut.

Puritans followed the teachings of CALVINISM.

Like other early Calvinists, the Puritans preferred a plain style of worship. They based their worship service on only what they read in the BIBLE. As a result, they did not allow artwork or musical instruments in churches. They also did not celebrate non-biblical holidays, such as Christmas.

Like most other Europeans at that time, Puritans did not believe in religious freedom. They believed that only people who met certain religious standards could be part of their colony.

The Puritans and their religious ideas have had very great influence on the United States. Many Americans believe that the United States has a special mission as a beacon of democracy in the world. The words in the Pledge of Allegiance, "one nation, under God," also echo the Puritan heritage.

CHOIRS, the smell and smoke of incense, and lighted candles characterize this style of worship. Orthodox Christians especially use special IMAGES called icons in their services.

On Sabbath, observant Jews rest and attend SYNAGOGUE. The heart of synagogue worship is reading from the TORAH scroll. It is kept in the front of a synagogue in a chest called an ark. Many synagogues remove the Torah scroll from the ark and parade it through the congregation in joyful procession before the reading.

Heroes and Saints. The first American who the Roman Catholic church recognized as a SAINT was Mother Elizabeth Ann Seton (1774–1821, canonized 1975). Born and raised in New York, she moved to Maryland, taught school, and founded an order of nuns. The northeastern United States has also been the home to many important Catholic archbishops and cardinals. The first was John Carroll, archbishop of Baltimore and the first Catholic bishop in the United States.

Religion and Immigrants in New York City

Most Americans are descended from immigrants. Immigrants are people who come from another land.

New York has many different immigrant communities. For example, New York has a very large Jewish population. One somewhat unusual example is the Lubavitch community in Brooklyn. Members of this community maintain traditional fashions. Men wear black coats and hats and long beards.

Immigrants from Cuba have brought a very different religion—Santeria. Santeria mixes the GODS of West Africa with the SAINTS of ROMAN CATHOLICISM. It has a rich tradition of art and music, too.

Hindus from India make up another immigrant community. They have brought their food, music, and fashions to New York City.

Religious diversity is seen throughout New York. For example, one can easily walk to synagogues, Hindu and Buddhist temples, and Chinese and Korean churches. In addition to these religions, several MOSQUES, including the Islamic Cultural Center in Manhattan, a Jain center, and a Wiccan fellowship help make New York the most religiously diverse city in the United States.

Many important Protestant leaders have lived in the northeastern United States, too. Thinkers known as New England Transcendentalists lived in Boston in the early 1800s. Among them were the writers Ralph Waldo Emerson and Henry David Thoreau. They had connections with Unitarianism. Some of America's most famous Protestant PREACHERS have also lived in the northeast. Examples include Jonathan Edwards, Phillips Brooks, and Harry Emerson Fosdick.

Some religious leaders who have lived in the northeast are probably unfamiliar to most Americans, but very important to their followers. Two examples from New York City are Menachem Mendel Schneersohn and A. C. Bhaktivedanta Swami Prabhupada. Schneersohn, the *rebbe*, or head of the Lubavitch Jewish community, moved his followers from Russia to Brooklyn, New York, as a result of World War II. Prabhupada, a retired chemist from Calcutta, came to New York City and founded the International Society for Krishna Consciousness—the Hare Krishna movement.

Architecture. The Puritans did not worship in churches, but in meeting houses. Meeting houses did not have steeples or ALTARS, and they were small. Inside they had a pulpit and benches. In the 1700s the benches were often changed into boxes where whole families sat.

In the 1700s, a style of church-building came to the United States that two architects, Christopher Wren and James Gibb, created in England. Many people now think of this style as the typical New England Protestant church. On the roof near its entrance stands a tall steeple and spire. A porch often marks the entrance and Greek columns usually support the porch roof. An example of this style is the Old North Church in Boston, from which Paul Revere made his famous ride. The Touro Synagogue, dedicated in 1762, in Newport, Rhode Island, has elements of this style, too. But it does not have a steeple.

The religious structures that are most distinctive of the northeastern United States are churches like Old North in Boston. But the region has many other kinds of religious buildings, too. St. John the Divine in New York City and the National Cathedral in Washington, D.C., are two of the biggest Gothic churches in the world. Hindus in the northeastern United States have built temples that reflect different building styles in India. Muslims have built MOSQUES, Buddhists have built monasteries and meditation centers, and many others have built their religious structures in the northeastern United States.

(continued from page 79)
spiritual has its roots in African American traditions. In the twentieth century, some people of African ancestry who came to the United States from the Caribbean, brought with them practices that combined African religions and Christianity, such as Santeria, VOODOO, and Candomble.

For the last 150 years, and especially since the 1960s, people from Asia and the MIDDLE EAST have been coming to North America. Some have adopted a religion from their new homeland. Many others have continued to practice the religion that they brought with them. These include HINDUISM, BUDDHISM, and ISLAM. Recently, these communities of immigrants have started building TEMPLES and MOSQUES throughout North America, especially in heavily populated areas.

It is sometimes difficult to have so many religions living together in one place. But North America has not seen any religious wars, as other parts of the world, such as Europe, have. One way North Americans have tried to avoid religious conflict is by keeping the government totally separate from religion. That has not been easy to do. For example, some people want religious activities, such as praying or reading the BIBLE, to be official activities of public schools. In the United States these activities would violate the First Amendment of the Constitution. [*See also* AFRICA (SUB-SAHARAN); EAST ASIA; INDIA AND SOUTH ASIA.]

NUNS *See* MONKS AND NUNS.

OCCULTISM

The use of a secret world by practices based on little-known religious knowledge. Some of these practices are astrology, fortune-telling, and calling upon spirits. People who practice occultism claim to have a secret knowledge of the hidden forces of the universe. Occult knowledge must be obtained either from people who already have it, or from secret books. Occultism often claims to be able to foretell the future and heal people of diseases by magical means. Forms of occultism are found today in NEW AGE RELIGIONS, VOODOO, WITCHCRAFT and Wicca, and in certain other practices. [*See also* MEDIUMSHIP; MYSTICISM; NATURE; SPIRITS; TRANCE.]

OFFERINGS

The objects given to a GOD in SACRIFICE. Some religions perform a special ceremony to kill an animal as an offering. But offerings may be many other things, such as food, money, or statues. Members of some ancient religions, such as the Aztecs, sacrificed, or killed, humans as an offering to their gods. Offerings are given for

In India, offerings are made before a religious statue.

various reasons. These include to praise God, to make a special request, or to thank God for an important favor. Today, offerings are often collections of money for the work of the CHURCH or religion.

OLD TESTAMENT ✴ *See* BIBLE.

ORDERS, RELIGIOUS ✴ A

particular religious group of PRIESTS, MONKS AND NUNS. Members of a religious order follow special rules for living and have distinct methods of serving God. For example, those in the Benedictine order follow the rule of St. Benedict. The Franciscans follow St. Francis' teachings.

ORTHODOXY, EASTERN ✴

A major branch of CHRISTIANITY. The Eastern Orthodox Church and the Roman Catholic Church split in 1054. The break came about be-

cause of differences in spiritual beliefs and political ideas. Members of Eastern Orthodoxy recognize seven SACRAMENTS. They also give special WORSHIP to icons, or holy paintings of Christ, the Virgin Mary, or a saint. They are known for beautiful and elaborate worship with fire music. The largest number of Eastern Orthodox believers are in Russia, parts of Eastern Europe, and Western Asia. Immigrants have established a strong Orthodox community in America. Orthodox Christians do not recognize the authority of the POPE. Their spiritual leader is the Ecumenical Patriarch in Istanbul.

His Holiness the Ecumenical Patriarch of Istanbul, Turkey

PACIFIC NORTHWEST

The states of Washington and Oregon make up the Pacific Northwest To the far northwest is Alaska.

The Pacific Northwest is unique in matters of religion. More people in Washington and Oregon than in any other state say that they have no religion. No one is quite sure why.

Of course, many people in the Pacific Northwest are religious. A little under one-fifth of the people practice ROMAN CATHOLICISM. There are a good number of BAPTISTS, Lutherans, METHODISTS, and Presbyterians. The Pacific northwest is not a center of JUDAISM, but some Jews do live there. Oregon may be the only state in the United States, apart from Hawaii, in which the second most widely practiced religion is not Judaism but BUDDHISM. (CHRISTIANITY is the most widely practiced religion in every state.)

The Pacific Northwest also has a distinctive Native American culture. It is closely related to the culture of native people living on the west coast of CANADA.

People who practice religions from Asia and the MIDDLE EAST also live in Washington and Oregon.

Alaska has a special religious history. Many Alaskans are Protestants, and Protestant Alaskans tend to be Presbyterian. Native traditions are strong, too.

Before 1867 Alaska was a Russian territory. Russian missionaries worked among Native Alaskans. As a result, Alaska has a number of EASTERN ORTHODOX churches.

Styles of Worship. Catholic, Protestant, and Jewish worship in the Pacific Northwest is much like Catholic, Protestant, and Jewish worship in other parts of the United States.

Worship in Orthodox churches is called the Divine Liturgy. Orthodox churches often use a Divine Liturgy that they say St. Chrysostom wrote. The most important Orthodox service is EASTER. It celebrates the resurrection of Jesus.

Like the Roman Catholic Mass, the Orthodox liturgy centers on the celebration of communion. Orthodox churches in Alaska have some surprising features. First, they have a great number of sacred pictures called icons. Second, although the Orthodox service has music, it does not have musical instruments. A CHOIR leads all music, and it sings without any accompaniment. Third, when people worship in Russian Orthodox churches, they never sit. They stand during the entire service.

A famous Native American ceremony from the northwest coast is the potlatch. At a potlatch, wealthy people gave away or destroyed much of their property.

Saints and Heroes. The Orthodox Church recognizes four Alaskans as saints. Saint Herman was one of the first missionaries sent from Russia to Alaska, in around 1800. The church says that he prophesied and miraculously healed people. It calls him "the Wonderworker of All America."

St. Innocent Veniaminov—"the Enlightener of the Aleuts and Apostle to America"—arrived in the

Religion on the Oregon Trail

Before the railroad was built, pioneers traveled to the Pacific Northwest on foot and by wagon. They often followed the Oregon Trail, which started in Missouri.

In a way, religion blazed the Oregon Trail. In 1831 Nez Perce and Flathead Indians from the Northwest turned up in St. Louis, Missouri. People thought that they had come to learn about CHRISTIANITY. So Roman Catholics, Methodists, Presbyterians, and Congregationalists sent MISSIONARIES to the Northwest.

In 1843 the first large wagon train traveled the Oregon Trail. A missionary named Marcus Whitman led them the last part of the way.

Until 1847, people traveling on the trail regularly stopped at Whitman's Mission.

In 1847, however, Native Americans around the Mission started to die from measles, even though white people did not. They suspected that the missionaries were somehow harming them, so they killed Whitman, his wife, and 11 other people. That was the end of Whitman's Mission.

Most of the people who traveled the Oregon Trail were Christians. Many had observed Sunday as a day of rest. But when the wagon train halted for a day, they had to do work, such as washing clothes and fixing wagons. But they did usually hold some sort of worship on Sunday.

Totem Poles

Native Americans on the coasts of the Pacific Northwest and British Columbia make totem poles. They carve tall tree trunks with large animal shapes, paint them, and set them upright.

People make totem poles for many different reasons. Some poles indicate who owns a particular piece of shoreline. Some are memorials for people who have died and may even contain remains of the dead. The carvings on some poles make fun of famous people who failed in some way.

Totems are symbols of traditional, Native American religions.

Aleutian islands in 1824. He became the first Orthodox bishop in America. Eventually, he returned to Russia and became the leader of the entire Russian Orthodox Church.

Two other saints are remembered because they died for their religion. St. Juvenaly was killed in Alaska because of his work with native people. St. Peter the Aleut, a Native American, was taken captive to San Francisco, California. There the Spanish tortured and killed him because he was Orthodox, not Catholic, and refused to give up his faith.

Native Americans of Washington and Oregon have also had religious heroes. One of them was Smohalla (ca. 1820–1895). Smohalla lived in the Columbia River area. He taught his followers not to plow the ground, as European settlers did, and not to buy and sell land.

Architecture. Visitors from elsewhere may be struck by the rich use of wood in church buildings and synagogues. They may also notice some influence of Zen Buddhism. One important example is a church that the architect Pietro Belluschi designed, the First Presbyterian Church in Cottage Grove, Oregon. It has a Zen-inspired garden.

CHURCH buildings of the Orthodox faith in Alaska and the Pacific Northwest are visually striking. Their shapes are said to symbolize the entire universe.

PACIFICISM ✤ The belief that war and violence are wrong. Some pacifists, or people who believe in pacifism, believe that all wars and violence are wrong. Others believe that only some wars and violence are wrong. These pacifists believe that certain evils are so bad that a war or violent act may be justified. Pacifists often refuse to serve in the armed forces. [*See also* BUDDHISM; CHRISTIANITY; HINDUISM; QUAKERS; WAR.]

The Life of Mahatma Gandhi (1869–1948 C.E.)

Mohandas K. Gandhi, one of history's greatest religious and national leaders. Gandhi was called "Mahatma," or "Great Soul," because his amazing words and actions seemed to come from deep inside. Gandhi was a pacifist. He led India to independence from Great Britain by teaching and practicing passive resistance. Passive resistance is nonviolent refusal to cooperate with injustice. Gandhi was a Hindu, but he also used Christian and Buddhist ideas and became an important inspiration for the nonviolent crusade of Martin Luther King, Jr. Gandhi sometimes practiced his nonviolent resistance by FASTING almost to the DEATH. He was killed by a Hindu who was against his nonviolence and his friendliness to Muslims.

PENTECOSTALISM ✤ A Christian movement that began in the United States at the beginning of the 1900s. Members of Pentecostalism work toward a religious experience called "BAPTISM with the Holy Spirit." This experience might involve healing an illness, making a prophecy, or interpreting a prophecy. It may also include "speaking in tongues," or being able to speak unknown languages in praise of God. Such experiences are recorded in the BIBLE as happening on the day of Pentecost. Pentecost is the Christian festival on the seventh day after Easter that recalls when the Holy Spirit visited the APOSTLES. The spiritual beliefs of Pentecostals are generally the same as members of FUNDAMENTALISM. Their services are often lively and include inspiring SERMONS and an energetic show of FAITH. At the end of the twentieth century, Pentecostalism was one of the fastest growing forms of Christianity.

PERSECUTION, RELIGIOUS ✤ The act of mistreating people because of their religion. Acts of persecution include burning sacred books, stealing property, or torturing and killing people because of their religion. Such mistreatment has happened throughout history. For example, in the early days of CHRISTIANITY, Christians were persecuted in the Roman Empire. Some religious groups are persecuted when they are a minority in their country. Perhaps the most horrifying modern example of religious persecution is the Holocaust. During World War II, 6 million Jews were tortured and killed by followers of Adolf Hitler, because of their religion.

Religious persecution was common in the 1600s.

PILGRIMAGES ❧ Special trips that religious people make to a holy city or place. During a pilgrimage, travelers perform certain acts that recall the historical or sacred events of their religion. For example, during the hajj of ISLAM, pilgrims drink

Hajj

The PILGRIMAGE to MECCA made by Muslims. According to Islamic law, every Muslim should make a journey to Mecca at least once in their lifetime if they are able. The pilgrimage begins with a ritual PURIFICATION. Pilgrims wear special white clothing or a traditional costume from their homeland. For the first part of the Hajj, a pilgrim walks around the Kaaba, the most sacred temple of Islam. Then they run between two hills to recall the desperate journey of Abraham's wife, Hagar. The main part of the Hajj is a series of RITUALS called the standing, the stoning, the SACRIFICE, and the feast. Each stage has special symbolic meaning and must be performed correctly, or the entire event will be invalid. When a pilgrim has completed the Hajj, he or she is called a Hajji. A Hajji earns special respect among Muslims.

water from a special well that helps them remember the same act by one of their ANCESTORS. People make pilgrimages to have a special religious experience. The journey helps renew their FAITH.

POLYTHEISM ✵ The belief in more than one god or divine being. SHINTO in Japan is a present-day polytheistic religion. Most ancient religions were polytheistic. For example, the Roman religion held that there were many GODS and GODDESSES who ruled over everything on EARTH. Most contemporary religions are *monotheistic*, or based on one god or supreme being.

POPE ✵ The Pope governs the Roman Catholic CHURCH, the largest body of Christians in the world. His office is called the papacy, and it has influenced the history of Europe for more than 1,500 years.

Pope John Paul II

The Pope, who lives in Rome, is said to be the successor of St. Peter, one of the APOSTLES of Jesus. Like Peter, he is the "vicar," or representative, of Christ on earth. The First VATICAN COUNCIL (1870) declared the Pope to be "infallible." This means that when the Pope makes official statements about what Christians should teach or do, he never makes mistakes.

A group of officials known as Cardinals help the Pope to guide the church. Cardinals also elect a new Pope.

PRAYER ✵ A personal message to a GOD or a holy being. A person says a prayer to ask for a favor, to ask forgiveness for a SIN, or to give praise. Some prayers are formally written, such as the Lord's Prayer in CHRISTIANITY or the Kaddish in JUDAISM. Some people who practice BUDDHISM say a prayer in which they repeat the same words, "Praise to the Buddha Amida," many times. Prayers may be said alone or with others in special places.

PRAYER GROUPS ✵ Groups of people who gather with the purpose of praying. A prayer group may be an informal gathering, such as a retreat or a Bible study group in PROTESTANTISM. In some religions, gathering as a group may be required. For

A prayer group in school

example, members of ISLAM must meet in a group for *salat*, or prayers, on Fridays.

PREACHER ✤ A religious person who gives SERMONS, or speeches on religious or moral topics. In some cases, a preacher holds a special office in his CHURCH. In other cases, a person feels a calling to preach religious ideas without a special office. Some talented preachers have become very popular and gained many followers. Some famous preachers have had great social and political influence.

PRESBYTERIANISM ✤ *See* REFORMED CHURCHES.

PRIEST ✤ A leader in many religions who performs or leads RITUALS. These rituals usually include offering SACRIFICES or mediating between God and the people. In ROMAN CATHOLICISM and some other groups priests can only be men. Catholic priests celebrate the Eucharist, or Mass. They can grant forgiveness for sins and teach the FAITH. Priests are also important in many other religions, including HINDUISM, BUDDHISM, SHINTO and many ancient religions. Most denominations of PROTESTANTISM call their leaders MINISTERS, rather than priests.

PROPHETS ✤ People believed to speak messages from God. A prophet issues a prophecy. A prophecy gives the word of God and may be a prediction of things that will happen in the future. For example, the book of Isaiah in the Old Testament is often interpreted as a prophecy of the coming of Jesus. Recent prophets include Joseph Smith who founded the LATTER-DAY SAINTS, and the Iranian prophet known as the Bab, who predicted the coming of the leader who founded the BAHA'I faith.

PROTESTANTISM ✤ A type of CHRISTIANITY that began during the 1500s as a protest against ROMAN CATHOLICISM. Forms of Christianity such as the Lutheran Church, the REFORMED CHURCH and the ANGLICAN Church are DENOMINATIONS of Protestantism. Each Protestant denomination has its own organization. Some have a national governing body, others have only local leaders. Most Protestant groups believe that

Martin Luther started the Protestant movement in Germany.

the words of the BIBLE are more important than tradition as a guide for living. Most also believe in the "priesthood of all believers," or that all believers have direct access to God. Protestant religious services usually include a SERMON, PRAYERS, and HYMNS.

PUBERTY RITES ✻ RITUALS performed when a child becomes sexually mature, known as reaching puberty. In traditional societies, a child becomes an adult at puberty, and rites are held to celebrate his or her coming to adulthood. Sometimes whole groups of girls or boys take part in these rituals. In some societies, the young person must go through tests to prove his or her adulthood. [*See also* BAH/BAT MITZVAH; RITES OF PASSAGE.]

PURGATORY ✻ In ROMAN CATHOLICISM, a place between HEAVEN and HELL. SOULS of sinners go to purgatory after death to be purged, or made pure, of small sins. After being cleansed from sin, the souls enter heaven. Catholics believe that a person's time in purgatory can be shortened if living people pray for them or do good works in their name. Purgatory is not part of the teachings of other denominations of CHRISTIANITY, such as PROTESTANTISM and EASTERN ORTHODOXY. Purgatory is not mentioned in the BIBLE, but it was defined by Catholic Church leaders at the Church Councils of 1274 and 1439.

PURIFICATION ✻ The process in which people or things are purified, or made clean, before they are worthy of God. Special purification RITUALS often use water, salt, or fire for purification. Most religions follow a purification ritual. For example, certain Native American groups purify their bodies by sweating in SWEAT LODGES. A special SHINTO purification ceremony is called *harai*. This ceremony removes dirt and pollution with water or by waving a purification wand.

QUAKERS ✲ A group of Christians also known as the Society of Friends. Organized in 1650, Quakers got their name from the quaking they would do when they communicated with God. Quakers are pacifists. They do not believe in fighting war. They believe that the way to find religious truth is to recognize God's LIGHT that shines in everyone. Most Quakers do not hold the usual Christian ceremonies during their services. They also do not practice the sacraments followed by other Christian groups. They meet silently during religious services until God moves a member to say something. One of the most famous Quakers is William Penn, who founded the colony of Pennsylvania in 1681.

QU'RAN ✲ The holy book of ISLAM. Muslims believe it is the word of God. The Qu'ran records the words of Allah as given to Muhammad by the angel Gabriel between the years 610 and 632 C.E. Soon after Muhammad's death in 632, all of Allah's messages were collected into one book. The Qu'ran was written in Arabic and Muslims be-

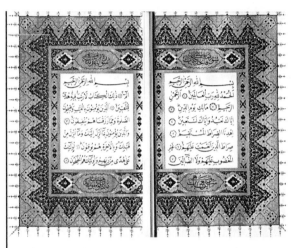

A page from an ancient copy of the Qu'ran

lieve it cannot be accurately translated into other languages. The Qu'ran says that there is only one God who is merciful and compassionate. The Qu'ran also says that Muhammad is the final prophet of Allah. It also tells about the earlier prophets sent by Allah, such as Abraham, Moses, and Jesus. [*See also* ANGEL; ISLAM.]

RABBI ✲ The RELIGIOUS AUTHORITY for a Jewish community. The word rabbi means "my teacher" in an ancient language called Aramaic. A

A rabbi reads from the Talmud.

rabbi is an expert in the TORAH and the Talmud—a set of books that records the stories and rules of the first rabbis. The rabbi has been the chief religious leader of JUDAISM since the destruction of the Temple in 70 C.E. Rabbis teach, lead PRAYERS, preside over ceremonies, and give people spiritual advice. Most rabbis work in a SYNAGOGUE.

REBIRTH ❧ The belief that people live many lives during their existence on EARTH. This process is called REINCARNATION. For example, followers of HINDUISM and BUDDHISM believe that a SOUL goes through cycle of birth and rebirth until a soul learns all it must know. Some religious groups believe that a person can experience a spiritual rebirth during their lifetime. For example, the RITUAL of BAPTISM is one of new beginning and rebirth.

REDEMPTION ❧ The escape from sin and from the punishment for sin. A sinner might achieve redemption by making a special SACRIFICE or by saying special PRAYERS. Christians believe that the life, DEATH, and rising from the dead of Jesus will bring redemption for all people.

REFORMED CHURCHES ❧ Protestant churches, such as the Presbyterian, that are based on CALVINISM, rather than on Lutheranism. They emphasize the power of God, so it is by His grace that people are able to go to HEAVEN, and nothing can be done to change that for those chosen. This is called predestination. People show their predestination by their FAITH and GOOD or bad actions. The Pilgrims who came to New England in 1620 and later, were in the Reformed tradition. It is because of their influence that the United States is regarded as a religious country. [See also CHRISTIANITY; PROTESTANTISM; SALVATION.]

REINCARNATION ⚘ A person's entry into a new body after DEATH. In HINDUISM and BUDDHISM, the new body can be that of a human being, animal, or plant, depending on one's KARMA. Reincarnation is not a belief of mainstream CHRISTIANITY, ISLAM, or JUDAISM. [*See also* AFTERLIFE.]

RELICS ⚘ An object that has been part of or close to a saint or holy person. Relics are especially important to BUDDHISM and ROMAN CATHOLICISM. Relics are considered sacred and are often kept in special boxes. Sometimes monuments are built especially for relics. Some relics are body parts, such as a tooth from the Buddha that is kept in Kandy, Sri Lanka. Other relics are objects that were important to a holy person. For example, some Catholic churches claim to have pieces of wood from the CROSS on which Jesus was crucified.

RELIGION ⚘ The belief and the WORSHIP of a sacred or holy power that has some control over human life. In most of American society, religion is separate from political or social parts of life. For this reason, a person's religion is often identified by what CHURCH a person goes to. In other cultures, there may be one religion for the whole society.

There are several elements that help describe religion. The first is worship. Worship is the love and admiration for a holy being or beings, as expressed in PRAYER or services. The second element is moral conduct. Moral conduct is knowing the difference between GOOD and EVIL and working to do good. The third element is right belief, or believing that certain teachings are true. Finally, part of religion involves the way it and its activities bind together families and communities.

RITES OF PASSAGE ⚘ RITUALS held when a person passes from one period of life to another. The most common rites of passage are celebrated at birth, puberty, marriage, and DEATH. The funeral is a rite of passage found in all religions. [*See also* FUNERALS; PUBERTY RITES.]

RITUAL ⚘ A pattern of actions in a religious ceremony that have sacred meaning. Rituals are formally described by the rules of a religion and each action in a ritual has special importance. Religious rituals often take place in special places or at special times. A ritual often recalls a historical religious event. For example, the rituals during the celebration of Passover in JUDAISM recall the time when the Jews were freed from slavery in Egypt.

SACRAMENT

A symbolic act and a set of prayers that bring a special grace or mercy on the person who receives it. Members of CHRISTIANITY believe that a special spiritual power is given during the ceremony of each sacrament. People receive a sacrament in ROMAN CATHOLOCISM and EASTERN ORTHODOXY when they are baptized, are confirmed, eat the holy bread and wine of communion, and receive forgiveness after confession.

A priest performs the sacrament of the Eucharist.

SACRIFICE

A special RITUAL in which something is given up to gain something valuable or to prevent something evil. Sacrifice is different in every culture. In ancient times, the most common sacrifice was the ritual killing of animals. Today many religions offer a symbolic sacrifice, perhaps bread and wine, during a religious service. Christians call the death of Jesus a sacrifice.

SAINTS

A holy person who has earned a special place in heaven for living a good life. Many saints performed MIRACLES during their lives on EARTH. In CATHOLICISM, people are named saints after their death. Certain saints are thought to have a special way to communicate with God. ISLAM also has saints. They are called *friends of God*. Muslims believe that a saint can act as a messenger to God.

SALVATION

An eternal reward, usually after death. Many religions teach their members to look forward to spiritual freedom from all that holds them back from full union with God. In this way, believers can live eternally with God.

SALVATION ARMY ✣ A Christian organization dedicated to helping the poor. The group was founded in England in 1878 by William Booth. It is structured much like an army with officers, soldiers, and divisions. The WORSHIP services are informal with free prayer and energetic singing. It also operates more than 3,000 hospitals, schools, and agencies for the poor.

SANCTUARY ✣ The area surrounding the main ALTAR in a CHURCH or religious building. It is a place for sacred RITUALS. Historically, it was a holy place where criminals would be protected from the law. The church would not allow a person to be killed in the sanctuary. Today the word can mean any place where a person or animal is protected from harm.

SATAN ✣ A name for the devil. Members of CHRISTIANITY believe that Satan is a fallen angel who tempts people to do evil deeds. They believe that Satan can only be overcome by belief in Jesus' SACRIFICE on the CROSS. For members of ISLAM Satan was the power that tempted Adam and Eve, God's first people, to SIN. They believe that Satan will be destroyed by their savior, Mahdi. Many religions believe that Satan is the chief torturer in HELL.

Jewish children attending Hebrew School

SCHOOLS, RELIGIOUS ✣ Special schools where people are taught the beliefs, practices, and traditions of their religion. Sometimes religious beliefs are taught by parents in the home, and sometimes they are taught by RELIGIOUS AUTHORITIES in houses of worship, such as Christian *Sunday school* or Jewish *Hebrew school*. Sometimes parents send their children to schools that combine nonreligious education, like math and English, with RELIGIOUS EDUCATION—how to perform RITUALS or how to understand SCRIPTURES. In the United States, these are called *parochial schools*. [*See also* TEACHERS.]

SCIENCE ✣ The study of nature by experiment and careful observation. Based on faith in things that cannot be seen or proven, religions explain the world very differently from science. Science and religion have often been in conflict. Hundreds of years ago in EUROPE, the scientist Copernicus presented his view that the SUN was the center of the universe. Up to that point, western religions had taught that the EARTH was the center of everything.

The creation of the world is often at the heart of the conflict between religion and science. Many religions see their god (or gods) as the creator of the world and all its creatures. A person who believes the world started this way is called a creationist. However, most scientists believe the Earth and its creatures have changed little by little, over millions of years. This slow change is called EVOLUTION. People who believe the world came to be in this way are called evolutionists. [*See also* FUNDAMENTALISM; HEAVEN; SKY.]

SCIENTOLOGY ⚘ A religion founded in the United States in 1954 by L. Ron Hubbard, a fiction writer. Scientology preaches REINCARNATION, and the preexistence of SOULS—the existence of souls before they enter the body of a new baby. The most important element in Scientology is Hubbard's "dianetics," a method he has created for healing troubled souls.

SCRIPTURES ⚘ A book or writings that are considered sacred by a religious group. The scripture of CHRISTIANITY is the BIBLE. The QU'RAN is the scripture of ISLAM. Members of religious groups usually believe that their scriptures were inspired by a spiritual truth. Scriptures often contain historical information, rules for living good lives, and wisdom about living fully.

SERMON ⚘ A religious speech usually based on a passage from SCRIPTURE. A sermon is sometimes called a homily. Many religious services include a sermon. For example, in ISLAM, Friday services include a sermon. Similarly, the Catholic Mass includes a sermon.

SHAKERS ⚘ A religious sect that formed in 1747. They got their name from shaking when they communicate with GOD. The Shakers came to America, following Ann Lee, in 1774. Shakers believe in CELIBACY among their members and thus do not have children. They rely on CONVERSION to increase their CONGREGATION. Shakers hold all property in common and treat men and women equally. Today there are few Shakers, but they are well known for their simple, elegant crafts and furniture.

SHAMANS ⚘ PRIESTS in native societies who use special religious knowledge for the good of the community. Shamans are thought to be the only persons to have influence with

SPIRITS, good or evil. And so they have great power among the people and are specially respected. One of their main duties is to heal the sick. Another is to tell what the gods say would be the best things for the group to do. For example, they often know where the best hunting will be. Shamans also conduct RITUALS, such as the RITES OF PASSAGE. [*See also* ESKIMO RELIGIONS; NATIVE AMERICAN RELIGIONS.]

SHINTO

The native religion of Japan. Shinto means "The Way of the Gods." The Japanese word for "gods" is *kami*. *Kami* are often associated with nature. For example, they may dwell in rocks, waterfalls, and mountains. But *kami* may also be the spirits of important people of the past. There are thousands of shrines to different *kami* throughout Japan. They may be found in cities as well as in the countryside.

Teachings. The basic Shinto belief is in the existence of *kami*. It is believed that if properly honored, *kami* can help in very practical ways. For example, *kami* can help students do well in exams and help people travel safely and stay healthy.

A very important *kami* is the sun goddess, Amaterasu. The *kami* associated with rice is Inari. Foxes are thought to be his messengers. There are often stone statues of foxes at Inari's shrines.

A traditional Shinto ceremony in which a baby is named

The Grand Shrines of Ise

At Ise, on the coast of Japan, stand two of the most important SHINTO shrines. They are known as the Grand Shrines of Ise. The buildings are very simple. They are made completely out of wood, and there are no metal nails. Every 20 years the shrines are taken apart and rebuilt. The new buildings are exactly the same as the old ones. This tradition of regular rebuilding has been going on since the eighth century, so we know what these Shinto shrines looked like 1,200 years ago. And they still look the same today!

Practices. If someone wants a *kami* to help them, they visit the *kami's* shrine. Shinto shrines are often in places of great beauty—in woodlands, on mountainsides, by the sea. One feature makes it easy to recognize a Shinto shrine, wherever it may be. At the entrance stands a special gateway with two or more cross-beams, called a *torii*.

Shinto festivals, called *matusuri*, honor and thank the *kami* of a shrine. A *matusuri* is a colorful event—often traditional Japanese clothing and special costumes are worn. The *kami* may be taken in a procession through the streets in a portable shrine.

After the procession people eat together near the main shrine. Musical and dramatic performances entertain the *kami*, as well as those attending the festival. [*See also* ANCESTORS; EAST ASIA.]

SIKHISM ❀ A religion that started in India about 500 years ago. It was founded by a man named Nanak. His message was simple: work hard and be devoted to God. Nanak was accepted by his followers as a spiritual teacher, or GURU. As a result, he is is often known as Guru Nanak. In India Sikhism is usually called Gurmat, or "the Teachings of the Guru."

Those who follow Sikhism are called Sikhs. The word *Sikh* means "DISCIPLE" and should be pronounced

Sikh priests, also known as *raggi*, performing prayers.

like "sick," rather than "seek." Sikhs have a strong sense of community. Sikh men are easily recognizable. Often they do not cut their hair but tie it up inside a special turban. There are about 16 million Sikhs in the world today. Most of them live in India. There are also sizable Sikh communities in Britain, Canada, and the United States, as well as smaller ones elsewhere.

History. Nanak was the first of a series of ten gurus. The teachings of these ten gurus are collected in the most sacred scripture of Sikhism, the Guru Granth Sahib. In this book there are many religious songs and poems of great beauty.

Over time Sikhs have become famous as fierce and brave fighters. This military tradition started because they had to defend themselves against persecution.

The Life of Nanak (1469–1539 C.E.)

Nanak was the founder of SIKHISM. He was born in the northwest of the Indian subcontinent, in an area called the Punjab. Nanak was born a Hindu. Yet where he lived, people were mainly MUSLIMS.

One day, Nanak felt he was taken into the divine presence of God. This experience changed Nanak's life. He felt he had seen the same truth at the heart of both HINDUISM and ISLAM. After his experience, Nanak preached a message of simple DEVOTION to God.

Teachings. Nanak believed that there is one universal God, who is also the Truth. He taught that the best way to approach God is through DEVOTION. All people—men and women alike—are capable of such devotion. So there is no need for complicated RITUALS or for PRIESTS to perform them. Sikhs believe in REINCARNATION—every person lives a series of lives. In the end, Sikhs hope they will cease being reborn in this world and dwell happily with God.

Styles of Worship. Sikhs WORSHIP by meditating on God's divine name. They also repeat it over and over again. In this way they get closer to God.

Sikhs also have temples, called gurdwaras. *Gurdwara* literally means "the door of the guru." There are no IMAGES in gurdwaras because God is believed to be formless. In the prayer room, which is the most important place in a gurdwara, there is a copy of the Guru Granth Sahib. Sikhs visit a gurdwara to sing devotional songs and listen to readings from the Guru Granth Sahib. They may also eat a meal together.

For Sikhs, worship is one way of serving God. Another way is honest work. Sikhs believe one can also serve God by serving others. They are encouraged to use one-tenth of their income to help those in need. It does not matter whether those they help are Sikhs or not. [*See also* INDIA AND SOUTH ASIA.]

SIN　An EVIL act, an evil thought, or evil words. In CHRISTIANITY and JUDAISM sin is an act against God's will. Most religions have a way to grant forgiveness for sins. For example, in ROMAN CATHOLICISM a sin might be forgiven when the sinner repents, or feels sorry, and receives the SACRAMENT of penance. Penance for Catholics might be to recite a PRAYER many times.

SKY　An important religious symbol in many faiths. Some people, especially those in ANCIENT CIVILI-

ZATIONS, have connected objects in the sky to gods or the divine. They might have believed that the SUN, the MOON, and the STARS were gods. Many faiths believe HEAVEN, a place where good people go after they die, is above the sky.

SNAKE ✺ A positive or a negative religious SYMBOL. Some cultures believe that snakes have good powers and can help human beings. Australian Aborigines believe that the rainbow snake is the creator and giver of culture. Other groups believe that snakes are evil and cause disaster. For example, in the BIBLE, a snake tempts Adam and Eve to eat the forbidden fruit, which leads to their banishment from Paradise.

SOUL ✺ The spiritual, everlasting part of a person. People in almost all cultures believe in the existence of the soul. They believe that the human body is temporary, but that the soul lives forever. In most religions, the soul is believed to pass to a life of everlasting reward or punishment after the death of the body. In HINDUISM, however, the soul is believed to be REINCARNATED. Many people believe that the soul is their real self, and that it is the part of a person closest to God or the gods. [*See also* HEAVEN; HELL; SPIRIT.]

SOUTH AMERICA ✺ South America stretches from Colombia and Venezuela in the north to Chile and Argentina in the south. In the late 1400s the Pope divided South America between Portugal and Spain. Portugal received the eastern part where Brazil is today. Spain got the rest.

Beliefs. Both Spain and Portugal are Catholic countries. Therefore, the official religion of most South Americans is ROMAN CATHOLICISM.

Many native peoples, sometimes called Indians, still live in South America. Many of them are Catholic, but they also practice religious traditions from their past.

Some people in Brazil have ancestors who came from Africa. Brazil has a religion with African roots known as Candomble. It is similar to VOODOO in Haiti and Santeria in Cuba.

In the 1900s Protestant missionaries started to work very hard in

The huge statue of Christ the Redeemer stands high in the mountains overlooking Rio de Janeiro, Brazil.

Religious Ferment in Brazil

In 1910 the first missionaries from a new kind of CHRISTIANITY called Pentecostalism came to Brazil. Since then Pentecostalism has become the fastest-growing form of Christianity in Brazil.

Like other Pentecostals, Brazilian Pentecostals have an experience that God's Spirit is taking them over. They believe that they should try to become holy, and that if they do, God will bless them with money and other good things.

These beliefs lead Pentecostals to change their lives in ways that other Brazilians find unusual. (Some North Americans may not find these changes unusual at all.) They give up drinking alcohol. They give 10 percent or more of their money to the church. They work hard to recruit new members. Some even claim to have healed people by casting out DEMONS.

Pentecostal churches often start up in the poorest areas. Some people criticize them for taking money from the poor. Recently, however, a Catholic charismatic movement similar to Pentecostalism has begun to grow in Brazil, too.

South America. They converted people to EVANGELICALISM and PENTECOSTALISM.

Styles of Worship. Native peoples do not all have the same beliefs. But most native peoples believe in "spirit beings" that make animals and plants live. Native people who are Catholics often believe in these beings, but they may prefer to call them SAINTS rather than "spirits." Native people who have become evangelical Christians often believe in these beings, too, but they call them devils. Native people traditionally believe that spirit beings give them what they need to live. Through RITUALS they give OFFERINGS back to the spirit beings.

In addition, Catholic priests celebrate the Mass in South America, as they do in other parts of the world. Protestant worship services take forms familiar in NORTH AMERICA.

Ethics. South Americans have used religion to try to solve several ethical problems. Starting in the 1960s some Catholic and Protestant religious leaders developed a way of thinking known as "liberation theology." It emphasized helping the poor.

Art and Architecture. South American Christians have produced well-known art and architecture. One of the most famous sculptures in all of South America is the large statue of Cristo Redentor—Christ the Redeemer—high atop Corcovado Mountain above Rio de Janeiro, Brazil. A landmark, it stands 125 feet tall and weighs more than 1,100 tons.

SPIRIT ✢ A supernatural being, like an angel, or the non-physical part of a human being that survives death. Spirits play a very important role in religions all over the world. For example, Christians believe that the spirit, or soul, goes to either HEAVEN or HELL. Hindus believe that the human spirit is reincarnated, returning to Earth as another person. [See also ANIMISM; CHRISTIANITY; HINDUISM; REINCARNATION.]

STAR ✢ Important religious SYMBOLS for cultures all over the world. Stars often represent GODS or mythical heroes. For example, the ancient Greeks and Romans told stories of heroic people and animals turning into stars and living forever. Other ancient people believed that the dead went to the stars. Christians believe that when Jesus was born, a bright star shown in the sky and lead the three wise men to Bethlehem. [See also ANIMISM; CIVILIZATIONS; ANCIENT; MESSIAH.]

SUFFERING ✢ Physical or mental pain interpreted religiously. Suffering is often viewed in different ways by religion. It can be seen as a punishment sent by God or a god. It can also be seen as a test, or as part of a process that will bring a greater good. For Christians, the suffering of Jesus Christ on the cross brought about the salvation of the world. The Buddha went through great suffering before attaining full enlightenment.

SUN ✢ A central religious SYMBOL throughout history. Many cultures worshiped sun GODS. The ancient Egyptian sun god, Re, was the most important of all their gods. Some Roman groups celebrated a feast on December 25 dedicated to the sun. Eventually Christians made this date Christmas, the birthday of Jesus. Creation MYTHS almost always mention the creation of the sun.

SUTRAS ✢ Stories, proverbs, moral rules, and rituals of HINDUISM and BUDDHISM. Both Hindu and Buddhist sutras were originally passed on by word of mouth. There are thousands of Hindu sutras, all taken from the VEDAS. Buddhist sutras are stories, especially the reports of the Buddha's sermons and conversations. Buddhist scholars have written a great deal to explain them. [See also EAST ASIA; INDIA AND SOUTH ASIA.]

SWEAT LODGES ✢ Huts or other dome-shaped enclosures used by North American native peoples
(continues on page 112)

SOUTHERN UNITED STATES

The southern United States stretches from Virginia south to Florida and west to Texas. It has a very distinct religious culture. Some people refer to this region as the "Bible belt."

The southern United States is the stronghold of BAPTISTS. Not all southerners are Baptists. Many are METHODISTS. In Louisiana almost half of the people are ROMAN CATHOLICS. In Arkansas and surrounding states, PENTECOSTALS are strong. But Baptists have a stronger influence in the southern United States than in any other region. They make up about half of the population of Alabama, Mississippi, Georgia, and North and South Carolina.

For many years, the southern United States was segregated. This means that African Americans and whites were kept apart. For example, African Americans could not attend the same schools or use the same drinking fountains as whites. African Americans often had their own churches, too, such as those belonging to the African Methodist Episcopal (A.M.E.) denomination. Like black Baptist and Presbyterian denominations, the A.M.E. Church started in the northern United States after the Revolutionary War.

United States courts have now declared forced segregation illegal. Nevertheless, predominantly white and predominantly African American churches still continue to exist.

Styles of Worship. Baptists emphasize the BIBLE. Many are FUNDAMENTALISTS. They believe that every word of the Bible is literally true.

For Baptists and many other Christians in the southern United States the most important part of worship is the SERMON. A preacher stands in front of a group of people and explains to them what the Bible teaches and how they should live.

The southern United States is also home to many revivals. A revival is a meeting or group of meetings with a visiting preacher or preachers. Sometimes big revivals take place in football and baseball stadiums. Revivals use music, PRAYER, and preaching to arouse people's emotions for religious purposes. People who attend revivals sometimes say they feel like new people. They are "born again."

Many southern Christians worship in these ways, but not all southerners do. Jews observe Sabbath. Hindus visit temples. Catholics go to Mass. In New Orleans there is a special celebration called MARDI GRAS. It marks the time before a period Christians call Lent.

Ethics. Christians in the southern United States have traditionally been very concerned with ethics. Some people say that this concern comes from the Civil War. After the

The Life of Martin Luther King, Jr. (1929–1968 C.E.)

Martin Luther King, Jr., is one of the most famous Americans of the twentieth century. He was born in Atlanta and grew up to be a Baptist minister, like his father.

While King was pastor of a church in Montgomery, Alabama, he became the leader of a movement that eventually did away with racial segregation. His method for doing so, "nonviolent resistance," became famous. He taught his followers that no matter what their enemies did, they should not fight back with violence.

King's most famous moment is his "I Have a Dream" speech, which he gave on the steps of the Lincoln Memorial in Washington, D.C., in 1963. As a result of King's work, the U. S. Congress passed laws to protect the civil rights and voting rights of all Americans. King received the Nobel Peace Prize in 1964.

King was shot and killed on April 4, 1968. Americans remember his contributions every year on the third Monday in January.

Civil War the southern United States was in shambles. People who lived there stressed ethics as a way to create order. For example, after the Civil War, southerners worked hard to make alcohol illegal, because they saw it as harmful to social order.

Southerners see the family as very important, and many southerners care a great deal about "family values." They generally have very traditional images of what a family is. In the 1980s and 1990s a group called the "Christian Right" championed family values. It worked throughout the United States, but its base was in the South.

Heroes and Saints. The best known religious leader from the southern United States is an African American minister, the Rev. Dr. Martin Luther King, Jr. Dr. King was originally from Atlanta. He dedicated his life to putting an end to segregation.

Another prominent southern religious leader has been Rev. Billy Graham. Rev. Graham was originally from North Carolina. Like Dr. King, Rev. Graham is a Baptist preacher. He has held revivals, which he calls "crusades," all over the world. In addition to holding crusades, he has used radio, television, and newspapers to spread God's Word—the message of Christianity. He has so much respect that several Presidents have asked him to visit them in the White House.

Music. The southern United States has had a big impact on American music. One important place for southern music is New Orleans. It is the home of jazz. Jazz is not actually religious music. But in New Orleans jazz FUNERALS are famous. A band goes with the family and the casket to the funeral service or burial. It plays slow, sad music. After the burial, the band strikes up energetic, happy music, and the mourners dance through the streets and party.

The southern United States also developed music that is more directly religious. At revivals and camp meetings people sang spirituals. These were folk-songs, that is, popular songs that were not written by someone trained in composing music. Black spirituals reflect the African American experience. They often talk about suffering and the hope of deliverance.

A festive Mardi Gras parade celebrates Carnival on the day before Lent.

Another kind of religious music grew up in the nineteenth century—gospel music. Unlike the spiritual, gospel music was composed or written by specific, named composers. In general, gospel music always has a harmony and instruments accompanying it. It, too, has made a big contribution to American culture.

Mardi Gras in New Orleans

"Mardi Gras" means "fat Tuesday" in French.

Before EASTER many Christians observe a period known as Lent, when they give up pleasures. Mardi Gras is the day before Lent begins, and the end of a period known as Carnival. Roman Catholics all over the world celebrate it with parties.

The biggest celebration in the United States is in New Orleans. People celebrate Carnival in two ways. First, private clubs, called *krewes*, hold balls for dancing. Krewes also sponsor parades. People ride on floats and throw beads and coins to the crowd. Mardi Gras is an example of how American secular culture can take over a celebration that was religious.

SOUTHWESTERN UNITED STATES

The southwestern part of the United States—the states of California, Nevada, Utah, Colorado, Arizona, New Mexico, and parts of Texas—combines some of the oldest and newest aspects of American culture and religion. For example, the Pueblo dwellings of New Mexico, such as the famous "sky city" of Acoma, built atop a high mesa, are probably the oldest continuously inhabited towns in what is now the United States. Among the newest examples are the "drive-in" churches, often found in California, where people stay in their cars during worship.

Festivals. The Native Americans who lived in Pueblo dwellings were farmers. They practiced religion based on the farmer's year—planting and harvest and the coming and going of the RAIN. They did dances wearing masks that represented the *kachinas*, or spirits of ancestors and gods who who brought blessings to the earth, especially rain and good crops. Some of this RITUAL is still practiced today. Beginning in the 1500s, missionaries, accompanying Spanish armies of conquest, began working in the American southwest and introduced Catholicism to the Pueblo people and other Native Americans in the area. This changed the nature of the people's ancient FESTIVALS.

Architecture. The Spanish built many missions, communities centered around a church and school, in which people lived and worked under the direction of Spanish PRIESTS. The most famous missions are found in California. Twenty-one missions, the first nine of which were founded by the energetic missionary Junípero Serra between 1769 and 1784, follow the Pacific coast. Mission churches are splendid examples of Spanish ARCHITECTURE of the baroque era, with a dim candlelit interior, an elaborate ALTAR in front, and walls covered with brightly colored statues of SAINTS and ANGELS. The Spanish heritage, represented today by buildings in this style and the presence of a large population of Hispanic descent, remains very important in southwestern culture.

Spanish-style architecture is shown in this mission church in San Diego, California.

In 1848, following the Mexican-American War, settlers of Anglo-American descent, largely Protestant Christians at first, began to come to this region. Mormons, or members of the Church of Jesus Christ of Latter-Day Saints, began to settle in Utah in 1847, establishing a community centered around an impressive temple in Salt Lake City. As time went on, Roman Catholics, Jews, and Eastern Orthodox also settled in the southwest and erected houses of worship that looked like European churches and synagogues.

In Texas, the traditional religions of the American south, predominantly Baptist or Protestant, mingle with Latino culture and its historical Roman Catholicism. Texas' most famous building, the Alamo in San Antonio where some 200 Anglo-Texan fighters were killed by a Mexican army in 1836, was originally a Franciscan Roman Catholic mission. Texas is today home to several important Protestant colleges and universities.

California, the region's most populous state, faces across the Pacific toward Asia. Chinese workers came to California in the middle of the nineteenth century. Asians have immigrated to this region in large numbers, and the culture and religious influence of Asia is seen in beautiful Hindu and Buddhist temples. These buildings might make

Spanish Missions

Many travelers to the American southwest visit the graceful missions founded in the 1600s by Jesuit and Franciscan missionaries from Spain. Missions were intended to convert the Native Americans to Catholic CHRISTIANITY, and to serve as centers of Spanish culture and control.

Some of the best-known Californian cities derive their names from the missions: San Francisco (St. Francis), San Diego (St. James), and Los Angeles, originally El Pueblo de Nuestra Senora la Reina de Los Angeles (The Town of Our Lady the Queen of the Angels). The safety provided by the buildings encourages swallows and doves to frequent the old missions. The missions remain a significant part of southwestern history.

one feel one was in India, Thailand, China, or Japan. Muslim immigrants have built several fine mosques. These very different places of worship—Spanish-style Roman Catholic churches, trim white New England or southern-style Protestant churches, and eastern European-style Jewish synagogues, among others—often appear side by side.

Styles of Worship. One characteristic of religion in the southwest is its many different forms. Especially in California, virtually every religion in the world can be found, often in large numbers. That state has also been host to NEW RELIGIOUS MOVEMENTS, many of which have originated or prospered there, and then spread elsewhere. These movements include new styles of Christianity, like Pentecostalism, with members "speaking in tongues" and engaging in lively singing and preaching. Other groups emphasize MEDITATION based on eastern teachings or revivals of ancient pagan religions. Some places, like Sedona, Arizona, have become known as centers of NEW AGE RELIGION. So many new religions may have arisen in California partly because many people, after long journeys spent crossing the seas or the deserts, wanted to break with their traditions and find something new for their spiritual lives.

Within some traditional religious groups, people have experimented with new ways of being religious. Some Buddhist churches in California, for example, have developed a Sunday morning service that adapts the Protestant style of service, with hymns and a sermon, to BUDDHISM. Some new Protestant groups use rock MUSIC and DANCE in worship. There are also services on

Religions in Los Angeles

Los Angeles, the largest city in California, is one of the most religiously varied cities in the world. Large and beautiful Roman Catholic churches reflect its Spanish heritage. Some Pentecostal churches are new Christian movements using contemporary music. At the same time, ancient Eastern Orthodox churches serve large Russian, Armenian, Greek, and other communities. The Jewish population in Los Angeles is old and well established. Its temples and synagogues are landmarks on some of the city's busiest streets. Large and imposing Buddhist and Hindu temples attract many visitors. All in all, Los Angeles is a city in which people of many religions live together.

the beach, where people worship in the open air. Overall, religion in the southwest is noted for experimentation, tolerance of others, and openness to new personal religious experiences. [*See also* BUDDHISM; CHRISTIANITY; FARMING SOCIETIES; HINDUISM; JUDAISM; NATIVE AMERICAN RELIGIONS.]

(continued from page 105)

Native Americans in front of a traditional sweat lodge

for ritual steam baths. The inside of a sweat lodge is very hot and steamy, so people sweat and remove any uncleanliness from their bodies. They also pray and sing. [*See also* ANCESTORS; NATIVE AMERICAN RELIGIONS; NORTH AMERICA.]

SYMBOL ✿ An object that represents or stands for something else. Religious symbols exist all over the world. The CROSS is a symbol for CHRISTIANITY. The Star of David is a symbol for JUDAISM. The Star and Crescent is a symbol for ISLAM. The TOTEM pole is a symbol for a Native American's spiritual ancestry. [*See also* NATIVE AMERICAN RELIGIONS; SPIRITS.]

SYNAGOGUE ✿ The place where Jews pray and commemorate Jewish FESTIVALS, celebrations, and HOLIDAYS, usually presided over by a RABBI. Synagogues are also places for religious study and serve as community centers. The most important part of a synagogue is the Ark, where the sacred scrolls called the TORAH are stored.

Synagogue comes from the Greek word meaning assembly or congregation. It was the name given to Jewish communities in the ancient world. After the second temple in Jerusalem was destroyed by the Romans in 70 A.D., Jews began meeting in local buildings, which they called synagogues. Today many also use the word *temple* to mean the same thing. [*See also* JUDAISM; RABBI.]

Temple Emanu-El in New York

T-V

TABOO ❧ A prohibition. The word *taboo* comes from a Polyesian word *tapu*, which means forbidden. A taboo may include a prohibition against touching or seeing something or someone, or a taboo may prevent people from going to a certain place. Many religious traditions have laws that include taboos. For example, Jews and Muslims are forbidden to eat pork. By tradition, native Australian men are forbidden to meet their mothers-in-law. Taboos are a way to help keep order in a socieity. [*See also* FOOD.]

TALMUD ❧ *See* RABBI.

TAOISM ❧ A Chinese religion and philosophy that started in ancient China about 2,500 years ago. Taoism gets its name from the word *tao*, which means "way." According to Taoism, the *tao* is the "way" to live if one wants to be happy.

Those who follow Taoism are called Taoists. In particular, Taoists aim for a long and healthy life. They try to achieve this by living in harmony with nature and the universe. The ultimate goal of Taoism is to become an immortal. Immortals—those who have become one with the *tao*—exist in special worlds, separate but connected to ours. According to tradition, the founder of Taoism is Lao Tzu, who is said to have lived in the sixth century B.C.E.

Taoists may also follow CONFUCIANISM or practice BUDDHISM because in some Asian countries, people do not choose just one tradition.

Lao Tzu rides a water buffalo.

Taoism is part of the richness and color of Chinese culture wherever Chinese communities are found.

History. Over time Taoism grew into a complex religious tradition. Taoists built TEMPLES where the immortals could be worshiped. Taoist priests developed RITUALS to help harmonize themselves and others with the *tao*.

Teachings. Some Taoists say the *tao* cannot really be described in words. It is too mysterious. Usually, however, one thing is agreed upon—the *tao* is the power underlying the universe. Everything is born from the *tao*. And as everything grows, the *tao* nourishes it.

Taoists believe that each person is unique. The problem facing people, according to Taoism, is that they do not allow themselves to grow naturally. They try to become someone or something that they are not. Taoism teaches that each person should be true to their uniqueness. How is this to be done? By living in harmony with the *tao*.

The Life Lao Tzu (Sixth century B.C.E.)

Lao Tzu is the traditional founder of TAOISM. His name means "Old Master." He is said to have lived at the same time as Confucius, the founder of CONFUCIANISM. There is a story that the two men met. Confucius was very impressed with Lao Tzu's wisdom. He compared him to a dragon that rides the wind in complete freedom. In fact, very little is known for certain about Lao Tzu. Some wonder whether he lived at all. But Taoists believe he did exist and that he is now one of the immortals.

According to the stories, Lao Tzu lived a simple life. He worked for ancient China, looking after the government's documents and records.

When he was older Lao Tzu decided to leave China. He wanted to live out the rest of his days somewhere more peaceful. So he traveled west, toward present-day Tibet, riding a water buffalo. The story tells that at the border he was stopped. The border guard, seeing he was leaving, asked Lao Tzu to write down his teachings. So Lao Tzu sat and wrote the *Tao Te Ching*, "The Classic on the Way and its Power," possibly the most famous Taoist book. Lao Tzu then continued on his way and was never heard from again.

Practices. Taoists use a number of methods to live in harmony with the *tao*. Taoist HERMITS live a simple life in the quiet of nature, away from the noise of cities—perhaps on a mountainside. Some Taoists work to transform their physical energies, for example, by practicing breath control. Others practice meditation.

TEACHERS ⚜ People who give religious instruction. The religious teacher, like the RABBI in JUDAISM or the GURU in HINDUISM, has an important role in passing on the FAITH from one generation to the next. Often this teacher is seen as the last in a line of teachers. These teachers hold special authority that is passed down from one to another.

TEMPLES ⚜ Special buildings in which people offer WORSHIP and PRAYERS. God or the GODS are thought to dwell in temples usually near an ALTAR. Some temples are very plain and simple. Others are very grand, with a great many decorations. Temples are found all over the world. Some of them are thousands of years old, while others have been built in the recent past. Buddhists, Conservative Jews, Shintoists, Sikhs, and some Hindus are among those who worship in temples. [*See also* ART, RELIGIOUS; BUDDHISM; HINDUISM; JUDAISM; SHINTO; SIKHISM.]

TEN COMMANDMENTS ⚜
The ten rules traditionally regarded in JUDAISM, CHRISTIANITY, and ISLAM as having been engraved by God on two stone tablets and given to Moses on Mount Sinai. The Ten Commandments are first listed in the second book of the BIBLE, Exodus. They are listed again in the fifth book, Deuteronomy. The Ten Commandments are: (1) I am the Lord your God. You shall have no other gods before me. (2) You shall not take the name of the Lord your God in vain. (3) Remember to keep holy the Sabbath Day. (4) Honor your father and mother. (5) You shall not kill. (6) You shall not commit adultery. (7) You shall not steal. (8) You shall not bear false witness against your neighbor. (9) You shall not desire your neighbor's wife. (10) You shall not desire your neighbor's goods.

Moses receives the Ten Commandments from God.

Jews, Christians, and Muslims consider the Ten Commandments as God's law for today. Other faiths have similar rules. BUDDHISM teaches the Four Noble Truths and Confucians follow the sayings of Confucius.

THEOLOGY ❧ Religious philosophy. For example, in JUDAISM, CHRISTIANITY, and ISLAM, God's message is believed to be contained in the SCRIPTURES. Theology would ask and seeks to ask such questions as: Who is God? Putting together everything the BIBLE and Qu'ran say about Him, what do we know about God? What kind of character and power does God have? HINDUISM and BUDDHISM, too, have theologies of their Scriptures. Theology is taught especially in schools that prepare persons for the sacred ministry.

TIBET ❧ A region of Asia in southwest China. Almost all Tibetans are Mahayana Buddhists. Traditionally, all life in Tibet was based on religion. Until 1959, when a rebellion against China failed, its government was led by the DALAI LAMA and other monks.

TONGUES, SPEAKING IN ❧ The act of suddenly calling out words and phrases no one understands. Speaking in tongues usually happens in American Christian churches connected to PENTECOSTALISM. Speaking in tongues is considered by these Christians to be a blessing and a gift of the Holy Spirit.

TORAH ❧ The first five books of the BIBLE. *Torah* means "law" or "instruction" in Hebrew. The Torah is the most important part of the BIBLE in JUDAISM. It contains the main Jewish religious laws, including the TEN COMMANDMENTS. Several copies of the Torah are kept in every SYNAGOGUE, written by hand on large parchment scrolls, and kept in a special place, called the Ark. These scrolls are very precious to the Jews and are often richly decorated. [*See also* SCRIPTURES.]

A young man holds the Torah at the Ark at Temple Jeshurun Kehilath in New York City.

TRADITION ❧ The way things have been taught and done in the past. Following tradition is an important part of most religions because religious FAITH is seen as having been given in the past. For example, JUDAISM, CHRISTIANITY, and BUDDHISM began long ago in the time of Moses, Jesus, or the Buddha, and have passed on as a tradition since then. Following traditions make people think of their ANCESTORS and their traditional ways. Many people value traditional aspects of religion, such as the customs surrounding Christmas, Passover, or an ancestral festival.

TRANCE ❧ A state of semi-consciousness, similar to being half-awake. Trances have played an important role in religions throughout history. Some religious groups believe that PRIESTS or other religious leaders can make contact with SPIRITS amd GODS while in trances. A medium, or person who is sensitive to the spirit world, helps people communicate with spirits. For example, a Haitian VOODOO priest goes into a trance. A spirit then takes over the body of the priest or priestess and talks to everyone. Among other groups, SHAMANS use ceremonial music, like beating on DRUMS, to go into trances. [*See also* FASTING; MEDIUMSHIP; MYSTICISM; SPIRIT.]

TRINITY ❧ Three in one. In Christianity, the DOCTRINE that God is One but made up of three Persons, the Father, the Son (Jesus Christ), and the Holy Spirit, is called the Trinity. Other religions also have sets of three divinities. Examples include a father, mother, and child in many SHINTO shrines and Brahma the Creator, Vishnu the Preserver, and Shiva the Destroyer in HINDUISM.

VATICAN COUNCILS ❧ Meetings of Catholic bishops, or leaders in the Vatican, the headquarters of the POPE in Rome, Italy.

Roman Catholic clergy in St. Peter's Square in the Vatican

There have been two important Vatican Councils. In 1870, the First Vatican Council decided that the Pope did speak *infallibly*, or without any errors, on certain religious issues. The Second Vatican Council in the mid-1960s tried to make the Catholic Church more modern, so Catholics would not feel isolated. [*See also* SOUTH AMERICA.]

VEDAS ﯓ The oldest sacred writings of HINDUISM. Hindus think of the vedas as Jews and Christians think of the BIBLE. The Vedas were written at different times, parts of them probably between 1300 and 1000 B.C.E. The writers are unknown. They are mainly four long collections of hymns, ceremonies, and essays. These collections are: (1) the *Rig-Veda*, containing more than 1,000 hymns to the GODS; (2) the *Sama-Veda*, containing parts of verses from the *Rig-Veda*; (3) the *Yajur-Veda*, containing the words to be used in various ceremonies; and (4) the *Atharva-Veda*, containing hymns, chants, and spells. [*See also* HYMN; MAGIC; RITUAL; SCRIPTURES.]

VIRGIN BIRTH ﯓ In CHRISTIANITY and ISLAM, the conception and birth of Jesus to the Virgin Mary by a MIRACLE of God. Jesus is believed to have had no human father, Joseph only being his guardian. The main source of the teaching on the Virgin Birth is the Gospel according to Luke, Chapter 1. [*See also* BIBLE; INCARNATION; SUPERNATURAL.]

VISION ﯓ The experience of someone or something in a dream or TRANCE. The BIBLE tells about the visions of the PROPHETS. Muslims believe that the Prophet Muhammad received visions that allowed him to recite the Qu'ran, the Muslim holy book. Native Americans sought visions to help them find their guardian SPIRIT. [*See also* ISLAM; NATIVE AMERICAN RELIGIONS.]

VOODOO ﯓ A religion found mostly in Haiti, but also in the southern United States (especially Louisiana), Cuba, Trinidad, and Brazil. Voodoo is a mixture of Roman Catholic and African religion. Catholic elements include the worship of a supreme God and the use of candles, crosses, and the sign of the CROSS. African customs include drumming, dancing, and the worship of ancestors, SPIRITS, and the dead. Also included are African gods, who are usually thought to be the same as certain Catholic SAINTS.

W–Z

WAR ❧ Armed conflict between nations or groups within a nation. Some wars have been fought over religious differences. The Christian crusades against the Muslims in the Middle Ages were religious wars. So were European wars between Protestants and Catholics in the sixteenth century. In our own times, wars between India and Pakistan, and some wars fought in the MIDDLE EAST, have been mainly religious wars. Most religious wars are fought in the belief that God or the GODS are on one's own side. The reason for this belief is that people consider their own religion to be better than the religion of the other side. [*See also* CATHOLICISM, ROMAN; CHRISTIANITY; INDIA AND SOUTH ASIA; ISLAM; PACIFISM; PROTESTANTISM.]

WEDDINGS ❧ Celebrations of the RITE OF PASSAGE known as marriage. A wedding is traditionally celebrated as a religious event. It is

Wedding celebrations are a joyous rite of passage.

usually performed by an official of the couple's religion, such as a PRIEST, MINISTER, or RABBI. Wedding ceremonies differ greatly from culture to culture. In EASTERN ORTHODOXY, the newly joined couple circle the ALTAR three times, hand in hand, as a sign of their union in the sight of God. In HINDUISM, the couple circle the sacred FIRE as a sign of the earnestness of their commitment to each other. [*See also* BLESSINGS; FAMILY; RITUAL; SACRAMENT.]

WICCA ⚜ *See* WITCHCRAFT.

WINE ⚜ An alcoholic drink, usually made from grapes. Ordinary drinks, like wine, often take on special religious SYMBOLS for people. For example, wine is an important part of most Christian traditions. During the RITUAL of Eucharist, Christians eat bread and drink wine. They perform this ceremony to remember the evening before Jesus died. Jesus told his DISCIPLES to share bread and wine to remember him. [*See also* CHRISTIANITY.]

WITCHCRAFT ⚜ The use of magic and OCCULTISM to affect nature and society. Witchcraft can be either good or evil. It is found in nearly all traditional societies. In some societies, as for example in Africa, belief in evil witchcraft has made witch dotors needed, to spoil the work of evil witches. In early centuries, witches were not usually punished severly. But in the Middle Ages, Christians began to think many women had given in to the Devil, and many accused witches were burned to DEATH. Today, most people who practice witchcraft believe it is GOOD, not EVIL. An example is Wicca, a religion with both ancient and modern beliefs and practices. [*See also* FOLK RELIGION; WOMEN AND RELIGION.]

WOMEN AND RELIGION ⚜

Women have always been important in religious MYTHS as symbols of life and death, such as the Hindu goddess *Devi*. Many religious traditions, however, do not give women the same RELIGIOUS AUTHORITY as men. Catholic women cannot be priests, and in some Muslim and Jewish traditions men and women have different rights and responsibilities. Women have had minor religious roles, such as NUNS in CHRISTIANITY and BUDDHISM.

In modern times, some religious traditions allow women to hold important religious offices, such as PRIEST and RABBI; women can receive more RELIGIOUS EDUCATION and they are allowed to participate in more RITUALS. Women have even founded NEW RELIGIOUS MOVEMENTS, such as CHRISTIAN SCIENCE. [*See also* CHILDBIRTH; GODDESSES; HEROES AND HEROINES; NEW AGE RELIGIONS; SHAKERS.]

A Presbyterian minister preaches a sermon to her congregation.

WORSHIP ❧ Activity done to honor and praise God or superior beings. People who believe in God express their faith according to the traditions of their RELIGION. Worship is often done by a group of believers. It may include a religious service, DANCE, offerings, the singing of HYMNS, the saying of PRAYERS, and the reading or chanting of SCRIPTURES. Worship also suggests the reverent inner feeling that occurs from being part of the activity.

YEAR, RELIGIOUS ❧ The year as celebrated according to the calendar of a particular religion. The religious year is usually based on the events of the growing season. For example, in some religious traditions, a NEW YEAR'S CELEBRATION, follows a new harvest. This FESTIVAL is then followed by a number of other sacred times spaced throughout the year. Festivals celebrated at these times are sometimes in honor of a particular god, GODDESS, or SAINT. [*See also* AFRICA; CHRISTIANITY; CONFUCIANISM; FARMING SOCIETIES; GODS; HINDUISM; HOLIDAYS; INDIA AND SOUTH ASIA; ISLAM; JUDAISM; POLYTHEISM; SHINTO; SOUTH AMERICA.]

ZEN BUDDHISM ❧ *See* BUDDHISM; EAST ASIA.

ZOROASTRIANISM ❧ A religion that started in ancient Persia (present-day Iran). Its founder was Zarathustra, a man who lived about

1200 B.C.E. Another form of Zarathustra's name is Zoroaster. The word used for the religion is based on this name.

Those who follow Zoroastrianism are called Zoroastrians. Today there are about 130,000 Zoroastrians in the world. But Zoroastrianism was the major religion of the great Persian Empire more than 1,000 years (from 549 B.C.E. to 642 C.E.). Its ideas influenced JUDAISM, CHRISTIANITY, and ISLAM.

There are still Zoroastrians in Iran today, but more live in India where they are called Parsis (or Persians). The Parsis left Persia in the

Zarathustra, the founder of Zoroastrianism

tenth century to escape persecution by Muslims.

Teachings. Zoroastrians believe in a supreme creator GOD called Ahura Mazda, the "Wise Lord." They believe that the world is basically GOOD. But there is also an EVIL force present in the world. This is the spirit Angra Mainyu. So the world is a battlefield between good and evil, Ahura Mazda and Angra Mainyu. Zoroastrianism teaches that people are free to choose between good and evil. If they want to be happy, they should choose good.

Zoroastrianism teaches that after DEATH, each person is judged. The good go to HEAVEN, the bad go to HELL. Zoroastrians believe that good will eventually win on EARTH. A savior will be born who will defeat Angra Mainyu in a last battle. Then there will be a final judgment. Those who are saved will have immortal bodies as well as SOULS.

Practices. PRAYER is especially important in Zoroastrianism. A good Zoroastrian will pray five times a day—at dawn, sunrise, noon, sunset, and midnight. The prayers include verses composed by Zarathustra. Zoroastrians pray standing up, in front of a flame or FIRE. Fire is a SYMBOL of Ahura Mazda. Its LIGHT and warmth stand for his goodness.

Zoroastrians pray at home or at a TEMPLE. The PRIESTS of a temple look after the temple's sacred fire.

They also perform various RITUALS. For example, there is a ceremony to initiate young girls and boys into Zoroastrianism. This ceremony takes place sometime between the ages of seven and 15. Each boy and girl receives a sacred shirt and a sacred thread during the ceremony. The shirt is white, for purity. The thread has 72 strands, which stand for universal friendship.

Zoroastrians have a number of holy days. For example, No Ruz ("New Day") celebrates the beginning of the year. At this time Zoroastrians feast, give presents, and attend religious services. When they die, Zoroastrians do not bury or burn their dead. This, they believe, would pollute the earth or the fire. Instead, they leave them in a stone tower to be eaten by vultures.

The Life of Zarathustra (Thirteenth century B.C.E.)

Zarathustra, also known as Zoroaster, was the founder of ZOROASTRIANISM. He lived in ancient Persia (present-day Iran) more than 3,000 years ago, in about 1200 B.C.E. Zarathustra is often said to be a PROPHET—someone whose words are inspired by God.

According to traditional stories, when Zarathustra was born, he laughed. This was a sign that he understood the basic goodness of the world. When Zarathustra grew up he became a PRIEST of the old religion of Persia. At that time the Persians believed in many GODS and the importance of making SACRIFICES to them.

When Zarathustra was 30 years old, he had an experience that changed his life. One day he was bathing in a river and he saw a shining being. This being led him into the presence of God. Later, Zarathustra had other VISIONS of God.

Soon Zarathustra started telling others about what he had seen and learned. He told them that the name of God was Ahura Mazda. He revealed that the EARTH was a battleground between the forces of GOOD and EVIL. At first Zarathustra was not believed. He was persecuted and had to flee to another part of the country. Eventually, Zarathustra converted a nearby ruler to his beliefs and his teaching began to spread. Zarathustra died when he was 77 years old. Stories say he was murdered by an angry priest of the old religion.

Selected Bibliography

World Religions

Barnes, Trevor. *Kingfisher Book of Religions: Festivals, Ceremonies, and Beliefs from around the World.* New York: Larousse Kingfisher Chambers, 1999.

Bowker, John, ed. *Oxford Dictionary of World Religions.* Oxford: Oxford University Press, 1997.

Bowker, John, ed. *World Religions: The Great Faiths Explored and Explained.* London and New York: DK Publishing, 1997.

Breuilly, Elizabeth, Joanne O'Brien, and Martin Palmer. *Religions of the World.* New York: Facts On File, 1997.

Due, Andrea, et al. *The Atlas of the Bible Lands: History, Daily Life and Traditions.* New York: Peter Bedrick Books, 1998.

Ellwood, Robert, and Gregory Alles, eds. *Encyclopedia of World Religions.* New York: Facts On File, 1998.

Fisher, Leonard Everett. *Gods and Goddesses of the Ancient Maya.* New York: Holiday House, 1999.

Gellman, Rabbi Marc, and Monsignor Thomas Hartman. *How Do You Spell God?* New York: Beech Tree Press, 1995.

Gold, Susan Dudley. *Religions of the Western Hemisphere.* Brookfield, CT: Twenty-First Century Books/Millbrook Press, 1997.

Goldman, Elizabeth. *Believers: Spiritual Leaders of the World.* Oxford: Oxford University Press, 1996.

Hartz, Paula R. *Shinto.* New York: Facts On File, 1997.

Hartz, Paula R. *Taoism.* New York: Facts On File, 1993.

Hartz, Paula R. *Zoroastrianism.* New York: Facts On File, 1999.

Hoobler, Thomas, and Dorothy Hoobler. *Confucianism.* New York: Facts On File, 1992.

Kindersley, Anabel. *Celebrations.* Batavia, IL: DK Publishing, 1997.

Langley, Myrtle, and David Pickering. *Eyewitness: Religion.* New York: DK Publishing, 1997.

Lugira, Aloysius M. *African Religion.* New York: Facts On File, 1997.

McFarlane, Marilyn. *Sacred Myths: Stories of World Religions.* Portland, OR: Sibyl Publications., 1996.

Osborne, Mary Pope. *One World, Many Religions: The Ways We Worship.* New York: Knopf, 1996.

Penney, Sue. *Sikhism.* Austin: Raintree/Steck-Vaughn, 1996.

Ross, Lillian Hammer, and Kyra Teis. *Daughters of Eve: Strong Women of the Bible.* Bristol, UK: Barefoot Books, 2000.

Savory, Louis. *The Children's Book of Saints.* Melville, NY: Regina Press, 1986.

Singh, Nikky-Gunnder Kaur. *Sikhism.* New York: Facts On File, 1993.

Stack, Peggy Fletcher, and Kathleen Peterson *A World of Faith.* Salt Lake City: Signature Books, 1998.

Stoddard, Sandol. *Prayers, Praises, and Thanksgivings.* New York: Dial, 1992.

Sturges, Philemon, Giles Laroche, and Kathy Dawson. *Sacred Places.* New York: Putnam, 2000.

Wilkinson, Philip. *Illustrated Dictionary of Religions.* New York: DK Publishing, 1999.

Wilson, Colin. *Atlas of Holy Places and Sacred Sites.* New York: DK Publishing, 1997.

Religion in North America

Hartz, Paula. *Native American Religions.* New York: Facts On File, 1997.

Hevly, Nancy, Judith Bentley, and Pat Culleton. *Preachers and Teachers.* Brookfield, CT: Twenty-First Century Books/Millbrook Press, 1995.

Walker, Paul Robert. *Spiritual Leaders: American Indian Lives.* New York: Facts On File, 1994.

Buddhism

Baromi, Helen. *Zen Buddhism Encyclopedia.* New York: Rosen Publishing Group, 2000.

Demi. *Buddha.* New York: Henry Holt & Co., 1996.

Ganeri, Anita. *What Do We Know About Buddhism?* New York: Peter Bedrick Books/Contemporary Publishing, 1997.

Landaw, Jonathan, and Janet Brooks. *Prince Siddhartha: The Story of Buddha*. Somerville, MA: Wisdom Publications, 1996.

Wangu, Madhu Bazaz. *Buddhism*. New York: Facts On File, 1992.

Christianity

Bial, Raymond. *Shaker Home*. Boston: Houghton Mifflin, 1994.

Benge, Janet, and Geoff Benge. *Nate Saint: On a Wing and a Prayer*. Seattle: YWAM Publishing, 1998.

Brown, Stephen F., and Patricia Lynch. *Christianity*. New York: Facts On File, 1997.

Penney, Sue. *Christianity*. Austin: Raintree/Steck-Vaughn, 1997.

Hinduism

Ganeri, Anita. *What Do We Know About Hinduism?* New York: Peter Bedrick Books/Contemporary Publishing, 1996.

Kadodwala, Dilip. *Hinduism*. Stamford, CT: Thomson Learning, 1995.

Lochtefeld, James. *The Illustrated Encyclopedia of Hinduism*. New York: Rosen Publishing Group, 2000.

Stewart, Whitney. *The 14th Dalai Lama*. St. Paul: Lerner Publishing Group, 2000.

Vishaka, Jean Griesser. *Our Most Dear Friend: Bhagavad-Gita for Children*. Barger, CA: Torchlight Publishers, 1996.

Wangu, Madhu Bazas. *Hinduism*. New York: Facts On File, 2001.

Islam

Armstrong, Karen. *Islam: A Short History*. New York: Modern Library, 2001.

Gordon, Matthew S. *Islam*. New York: Facts On File, 1991.

Hasan, Asma. *American Muslims: The New Generation*. New York: Continuum, 2001.

Husain, Shahrukh, and Celia Hart. *What Do We Know About Islam?* New York: Peter Bedrick Books/Contemporary Publishing, 1996.

Penney, Sue. *Islam*. Austin: Raintree/Steck-Vaughn, 1997.

Judaism

Chaikin, Miriam, and Erika Weihs. *Menorahs, Mezuzas, and Other Jewish Symbols*. Boston, MA: Clarion Books, 1990.

Drucker, Malka. *The Family Treasury of Jewish Holidays*. Boston, MA: Little, Brown, 1999.

Morrison, Martha and Stephen F. Brown. *Judaism*. New York: Facts On File, 1991.

Morrow, Betty, and Louis Hartman. *Jewish Holidays*. (A Holiday Book). Champaign, IL, Garrard Publishing, 1967.

Schaffer, Patricia. *Chag Sameach! Happy Holidays*. Allen, TX: Tabor Sarah Books, 1985.

Weber, Vicki. *Tradition! Celebration and Ritual in Jewish Life*. West Orange, NJ: Hugh Lanter Levin Associates, 2001.

Zorn, Steven. *Little Book of Hanukkah*. Philadelphia: Running Press, 2000.

Index

Page numbers for main entries (including feature box titles) are in boldface. Page numbers for illustrations are in italics.